Teach Your Child to Swim

Teach Your Child to Swim

Susan Meredith

with Carol Hicks

Swimming consultant and Amateur Swimming Association staff tutor,
Crystal Palace National Sports Centre

and Jackie Stephens

Amateur Swimming Association tutor,
Crystal Palace National Sports Centre

Designed by Joanne Kirkby

Illustrated by Roger Fereday

With advice from the Amateur Swimming Association:
Alison Bell, Mary Bainbridge, Jean Findlay, Jean Cook, Lorna Hunt

Edited by Robyn Gee
Revision editor: Kirsteen Rogers
American editor: Carrie Armstrong
Series editor: Felicity Brooks
Cover designer: Francesca Allen
Cover illustrator: Dubravka Kolanovic

With thanks to:
Little Dippers and Waterbaby
and
Amateur Swimming Association

Farrah Dever, American Red Cross
Association for Spina Bifida and Hydrocephalus
The Royal Life Saving Society UK
Scope
Epilepsy Action
UK Deaf Sport
Down's Syndrome Association
The National Autistic Society
Diabetes UK
Asthma UK
RNIB

Contents

Teaching children to swim

Swimming is a very valuable skill to teach children. It helps them keep safe, it's an excellent all-round form of exercise they can do throughout their life, and it can be relaxing, exciting, therapeutic and, of course, fun.

One-to-one support

Research has shown that children make most progress in swimming when they're introduced to the water by a parent, caregiver or other adult they know well. The close one-to-one relationship makes it easier to build up their confidence, which is essential for learning to swim.

You don't have to be an expert swimmer yourself, or even to swim at all, to get children started, as long as you're confident walking in shallow water. All you should be aiming to do in the early stages is to enjoy being in the water together.

Using this book

The first part of this book has ideas for safe and gentle introductory activities. The emphasis is on allowing children to go at their own pace without putting them under pressure.

Once children are afloat, you can move on to the chapters that introduce swimming strokes and other water skills. You may be able to use these to improve your own swimming as well. As the children get older, you could work together to improve each other's performance. Older children might find it helpful to read the strokes and water skills sections for themselves, and you can encourage children of all ages to look at the pictures.

Close support from a trusted adult is very important for building up a small child's confidence in water.

When to start

Some people believe that after nine months in a fluid environment babies are born without fear of water and able to swim, so the sooner you introduce them to the water, the better. There are specific methods for helping very small babies learn to swim, and some of them have achieved spectacular results.

Current medical thinking is that you can take children into a well-ventilated swimming pool at any age (normally around four to five months), whether or not they've been immunized, as long as the water is warm enough. Psychologically, it's best if babies are used to going in the big bathtub at home before you take them to a pool.

The ideal age

For many babies, four to five months can be the ideal age to start going to the pool. By about six months they're usually starting to sit up and will try to do this in the water as well as out of it. By eight to nine months they're often becoming more fearful both of water and strange environments. In general, the older children are when they first start going swimming, the more apprehensive they're likely to be. That said, there's no point in going swimming early if you don't feel you're both ready.

Tip...

Once you start, try to go swimming regularly. Children learn much more in short, frequent visits than in occasional long ones.

Babies who are just learning to sit up often need extra encouragement to relax and lie flat in the water.

Keep it fun

The first step toward learning to swim is feeling at ease in the water, so it's well worth planning ahead to make sure a child's first experience of swimming is a happy one.

As children progress, remember that swimming should continue being fun. Although the different strokes and skills are explained in some detail, don't become too concerned with achieving the perfect style. Many of the best swimmers swim at least partly by instinct and wouldn't be able to analyze what they do. Improvement often comes naturally with plenty of progressive practice and, above all, continued enjoyment of the water.

In the bathtub

Bathtime provides a great opportunity to prepare babies and young children for going swimming. Washing them gets them used to feeling water on their head, face and body, and play activities during bathtime can help get them ready for future activities at the swimming pool.

Babies and water

Babies are used to moving their arms and legs around in a fluid environment before birth and will do the same when they're put in water soon after they're born, as long as they feel relaxed and safe.

As they develop, many babies and young children go through various phases in their attitude to water. Some babies feel insecure at first when their clothes are taken off, and many actively dislike bathtime at some stage. None of the activities shown here should be forced on children who aren't enjoying them. If children who were previously happy in the water suddenly become unhappy, just revert to earlier, gentler activities until the phase passes.

Giving reassurance

Always reassure babies during bathtime by chatting, smiling and singing to them. Remember to praise them often and maintain eye contact as much as possible. Keep the emphasis on fun and helping them to feel happy and confident in the water. Bathtime play also gives you the chance to become more used to handling a baby in water. It's important that you're confident with the activities, as babies sense this and find it reassuring.

Bathtime provides an ideal opportunity for babies to get used to being in water.

Safety...

Timing

The most practical time for bath play is at a baby's usual bathtime. Do it before you wash them, as soapy water can make them slippery to hold. Keep bathtime short to start with, then gradually lengthen it, taking your cue from the child. To start with, very young babies may stay in water of a suitable temperature for about five minutes. You can build this up little by little to 10–15 minutes by the age of three months.

Warm air and water

Bathtime provides children's first experiences of water so try to keep them as relaxed as possible, making sure they aren't put off by feeling cold.

For young babies the water temperature needs to be between 84°F (29°C) and 90°F (32°C). The water should feel warm to your elbow or the inside of your wrist. If you want to measure the temperature more accurately, you could use a thermometer. The bathroom needs to be warm too, with the temperature as high as 75°F (24°C) if you can manage it.

Bathtime activities

The next few pages suggest activities that can be used at bathtime. Many of them can be used in the baby bathtub, in the big bathtub and eventually in the swimming pool. By repeating activities at each stage, you can help children progress confidently to each environment in turn. Always build up the activities gradually, and make sure children are happy with one activity before moving on to the next.

In the baby bathtub

To support a baby in the bathtub, slip your hand behind their neck so their head is supported by your forearm and hold the top of the arm furthest away from you. Put your other hand under their bottom and lower them gently into the bathtub, keeping their head clear of the water. You can then take your hand from under their bottom and use it for some of the water activities described over the page and, later, for washing them.

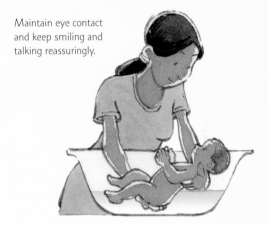

Maintain eye contact and keep smiling and talking reassuringly.

If the baby is happy in the bathtub, slip your free hand under their bottom again and then slowly lower their head until the ears are just submerged for a short time. Avoid this activity if the baby has sensitive ears or is suffering from an ear infection.

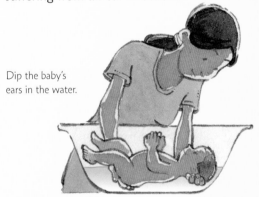

Dip the baby's ears in the water.

You may be able to take your hand from under their bottom and use it to attract their attention from above. This gives the baby something to look at and helps them to adopt a flatter body position in the water.

Swishing to and fro

Gently swish the baby backward and forward in the bathtub, with one hand under their head and the other under their bottom. Avoid letting water splash their face at this stage. Once babies have learned to sit up, at around six to nine months, they may show signs of distress when put on their back in the bathtub, and prefer to sit up.

Encouraging breath control

It's worth trying to get babies used to water on their head and face right from the start. Let them know that something is going to happen by saying something like, "Ready, go!" before you start. Babies learn to recognize this as a cue to hold their breath and not to suck in water. Without this cue, they might try to snatch a quick breath and start to cough or choke.

Use your fingers to sprinkle a little water over the baby. Start with their body and shoulders then progress to the back of their head. If they enjoy it, gradually sprinkle water farther forward on their head and let a little trickle over their face. Use the warning cue, "Ready, go!"

Tip...

Singing nursery rhymes or action songs to accompany activities such as sprinkling water, floating and swishing can help make the experience fun. Songs can also provide continuity if you repeat them when your baby transfers to a swimming pool.

Sponges, bottles and beakers

Use the "Ready, go!" cue and gently squeeze a sponge near the baby, to show what happens. Then squeeze it over their body, shoulders and the back of their head, repeating the cue with each squeeze. As they get more comfortable with the sensation, let a little water trickle over their face. Let them play with the sponge too.

Repeat the activity using plastic containers, such as bottles and beakers. Remember to give your cue before you start. Babies often enjoy playing with the containers too, and with other toys that squirt, sprinkle and pour.

Use sponges, cups and sprinkle toys to introduce babies to different sensations during their bathtime.

Preparing for the big bathtub

At two or three months old, some babies are ready to go in the big bathtub. This may seem vast to them, compared with the baby bathtub, so a good intermediate step is to put the baby bathtub inside the big one. This allows them to get used to the larger area gradually.

A non-slip mat on the bottom of the big bathtub gives extra security and protection, but it is still never safe to leave babies or young children unsupervised in the bathtub.

In the big bathtub

Once they are in the big bathtub, repeat the activities they've done in the baby bathtub. Keep using your cue and reassure the baby constantly by maintaining eye contact, smiling and talking.

Babies under about six months may float happily on their back with just a hand under their head.

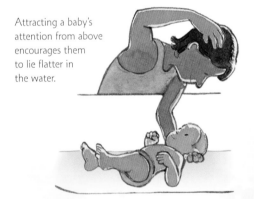

Attracting a baby's attention from above encourages them to lie flatter in the water.

As they get older, gradually encourage them to lie flat in the bathtub without support. The water must be shallow enough to come only halfway up their head, so their face is well clear of the water. Encourage them to kick by gently holding their legs below the knee and moving them up and down, keeping them as straight as possible and repeating the cue, "Kick, kick!"

On their front

At about three to four months, babies may also like lying on their front in shallow water. Support them from behind under their shoulders, with your fingers across their chest and your thumbs uppermost. Then move them gently to and fro, making sure their face stays clear of the water.

If the baby is too young to support their head, stretch your fingers under their chin to prevent their face from going in the water. Babies might curl their legs up under them to start with, but they'll gradually learn to relax and straighten out.

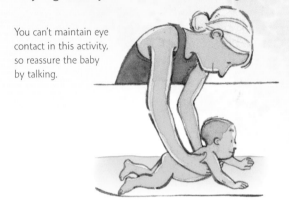

You can't maintain eye contact in this activity, so reassure the baby by talking.

Older babies or young children may enjoy walking their hands or forearms along the bottom of the bathtub while kicking their legs gently. They can do this on their back as well as on their front.

Sitting babies in the middle of the bathtub leaves room for you to support them from behind and keeps them at a safe distance from the faucet.

Water play

Once babies are able to sit up in the bathtub, give them a selection of toys, such as sponges and plastic watering cans or other sprinkle toys, to play with. Containers are good because they give babies the opportunity to pour water over themselves. Besides bath toys, you could give them plastic containers, spoons, ladles, strainers and funnels from the kitchen.

Encourage babies to splash with their hands by putting floating toys such as ducks in front of them and showing them how to push them along. Reaching out to play with toys helps develop their arm movements too. It's better to let them do the splashing, although they may enjoy you gently splashing their tummy or back.

Ears under

At each bathtime, encourage older babies or children to lie flat on their backs with their shoulders or, even better, their ears, under water. Afterwards, let the water drain from their ears by tilting their head to each side for a few seconds, and dry them with a towel. Avoid the activity if they have sensitive ears or an ear infection.

Blowing bubbles

Blowing bubbles in the water is an important skill as it's the first stage in learning to breathe correctly when swimming. This can be started in the bathtub at the age of 12 months.

Start by blowing bubbles across the surface of the water.

Once they can blow bubbles across the surface, get them to blow with their mouth under water, progressing to submerging their nose, eyes then face as they blow. Encourage them to keep their eyes open under water, by getting them to pick up small objects from the bottom of the bathtub.

In the bathtub together

Sharing a bath with your child, at the age of about two months, does a lot to build their confidence, especially if they're nervous of water. It's easier if a second person lifts the baby in and out of the bathtub. Start with familiar activities you've done in the baby bath and big bathtub then move on to the ones suggested here.

Young children can be encouraged in their bath play by sharing a bath with an older child. You'll need to supervise even more closely than usual, and it may be safer to avoid a shared bath at the stage when a baby is learning to stand up.

Supported floating

Sit behind the baby and hold them with your hands under their shoulders and thumbs over the top. Press your wrists and forearms together to support their head, and see if the baby is happy to float in this way. Small babies often float easily like this, but they stop floating so well once they can sit up because they try to sit up in the water. When they are comfortable in this position, slowly swish them to and fro, avoiding water flowing over their face.

Gliding and kicking

At the age of three to four months, you can lie babies on their front, face to face with you. Hold them under their arms with your wrists together to support their chin and keep their face out of the water, then gently glide them back and forth. Don't insist on doing this activity if they dislike going on their front. Next, let the baby lie in your lap on their back, hold their legs below the knees and move them to simulate kicking, repeating the cue, "Kick, kick!"

You may like to prepare babies for their first visit to a pool by putting a swim diaper on them, and wearing your swimsuit.

Babies may rest on your legs to start with: they'll probably stretch out into a floating position as they relax.

Tip...

If you are intending to put armbands on your child at the swimming pool, it's a good idea to let them try them on and play with them in the bathtub before they wear them at the pool.

Sharing a bath with your children is an ideal way to get them used to being in the water with you.

Finding a suitable pool

Swimming pool facilities vary considerably and it may be worth traveling a little farther afield than you otherwise would to find one with specially good facilities for babies and young children.

Access to the pool

Find out how easy it is to get to the swimming pool. Are there access ramps for strollers and wheelchairs? Check the public transportation system to the pool or, if you are going by car, find out how easy it is to get from the parking lot to the pool.

Teaching pools

Is there a separate pool for small children? These are often called teaching or wading pools and are usually about 3 feet (1m) deep throughout or graduated from 1½ feet (0.5m) to 3 feet (1m). The water is warmer than the main pools, and the atmosphere is usually more relaxed and inviting. Find out when the pool is open and when it is quietest. Babies and toddlers are likely to be upset or distracted by a lot of noise and activity. Before you go, it's also a good idea to find out whether swimming caps are required.

All non-swimmers need warm water, and it's essential for babies. They lose heat quickly, but don't have a shiver reflex, so they can get extremely cold very quickly, with no apparent symptoms until they start to turn blue. For babies and toddlers the water needs to be at least 84°F (29°C) to be safe, and is better between 86°F (30°C) and 88°F (31°C). By the time a child is three, 82°F (28°C) is enough. It is recommended that the air temperature is one or two degrees higher than the water temperature.

Tip...

Some swimming pools have information about temperatures on display to the public; if not, you could ask a staff member.

The warm air and water in teaching pools provide a relaxing and comfortable environment for adults and children.

Changing facilities

Are the changing facilities suitable for babies and young children and accessible by male and female caregivers? There should be changing mats or changing tables, bins for diapers, playpens or special chairs to put babies in while you get changed and non-slip matting on the floor. You may need to check whether the changing facilities are suitable for people with disabilities, with extra space, grab rails, a changing bed and a shower chair available.

Find out where the lockers are, and what (if any) the charge is for using them. If you plan to bring a stroller, wheelchair or car seat, check out storage facilities for these too.

Ideally, the toilets should be fairly near the pool, especially for newly potty-trained toddlers or children for whom continence management is an ongoing issue.

Water depth

If the water is shallow, between 1 foot and 1½ feet (0.3m and 0.5m), it's easy to get in and out. Some children find shallow water less intimidating as they can stand without using flotation aids and they're likely to be able to lie horizontally in the water without aids at an earlier stage. If there is an area of very shallow water, young children can sit, crawl or splash around. However, children may become too used to having their feet on the floor, and the constant bending down may cause back problems for some adults.

In deeper water, between 3 feet and 4 feet (1m and 1.3m), adults can usually hold children more comfortably and maintain eye contact easily. Children can try a wider variety of entries, such as jumping in, with and without adult support, and they may learn to swim earlier, as their feet can't touch the bottom. It may be more difficult to get into and out of the pool, though. Adults who are nervous of water may feel less secure and the water may be cooler, which can be off-putting. Children may need to use flotation aids for more of the time, and they may find themselves out of their depth more quickly.

Checklist...

✓ Access (parking, ramps, public transportation)

✓ Opening hours and public swimming hours

✓ Teaching pools (is equipment available or do you need to bring your own?)

✓ Water and air temperature

✓ Swimming cap policy

✓ Changing facilities (lockers, changing mats, playpens, disabled facilities, location of toilets)

✓ Water depth

✓ Access into the pool (steps, ladders or ramps)

✓ Fee or membership dues for pool use

Getting in and out

How do you get into and out of the pool? Some toddlers prefer to walk into the water rather than being carried. A gentle slope or wide, shallow steps are best for this. Wheelchair users may prefer a sloped entry, or need a hoist, which some pools have available on request.

This teaching pool is shallow enough for toddlers to walk confidently, and deep enough for them to try getting afloat.

What to take

A visit to the swimming pool will be a much more enjoyable experience for you and the child if you come well prepared. Here are a few suggestions of things you might need to consider.

Swim diapers or pants

Children who aren't yet potty trained will need to wear a swim diaper. These can be disposable or reusable, and come in various sizes and designs, from diapers with Velcro® or tie fastenings to pull-on pants. Most can be worn by themselves or underneath swimsuits.

For a snug leak-free fit, look for styles with adjustable waists and elastic legs. Babies are likely to be most comfortable in diapers made from breathable waterproof material.

Tip...

Try a new swim diaper on your child before you go to the pool to make sure it's comfortable and fits well.

The other thing to bear in mind when opting for a particular style of swim diaper is how easily you can remove it if the child needs a diaper change.

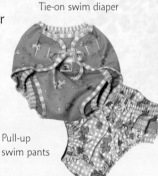

Tie-on swim diaper

Pull-up swim pants

Swimsuits

Choose something that fits well and is easy to get on and off. Look for styles that don't impede movement – swimming trunks, rather than shorts, are better for boys. Make sure your own swimsuit is comfortable and practical, too, and can't be tugged down too easily.

Towels and bathrobes

Wrapping children in a big, soft towel or bathrobe after they come out of the pool can help them feel warm and secure after their adventures in the water. It will also absorb any leaks while they're not wearing a diaper. A hooded towel has the added advantage that it keeps their head warm while you dry them. An extra towel can be useful, too.

Remember to pack towels for you and the child. The bigger, the better.

Bath toys

Bringing a couple of favorite bath toys to the pool can make children feel more at home. Toys can help them explore the properties of water by watching what floats and what sinks, or by enjoying splashing and pouring. They can also be used in activities that will help build up their confidence in water.

Encouraging children to reach out for toys is a great way to get them to stretch their arms.

Swimming caps

Some swimming pools require users to wear swimming caps. There are two main types. Rubbery ones (made of latex or silicone) are more waterproof, and stretchy cloth ones are more comfortable, and easier to get on and off.

Tip...

Children and adults with long hair should wear it tied back, to keep it out of the way, and to help keep the pool clean.

Goggles

It's best to avoid goggles for babies and young children as they aren't made small enough to get a proper fit. It can also be dangerous if children try to pull them off, as they can bounce back and hit the eyes. Goggles can be useful for contact lens wearers, and older children who spend more time in the water. Some people who wear glasses buy prescription goggles for swimming.

Sun protection

If you're taking children to an outdoor pool, make sure you're both adequately protected from the sun. Use waterproof sunscreen, sunshades and protective clothing as appropriate.

Checklist...

✔ Swim diaper and/or swimsuit

✔ Spare swim diaper

✔ Your swimsuit and towel

✔ Child's towel and hooded bathrobe

✔ Swimming cap (if needed)

✔ Flotation aid (if needed)

✔ Tissues for wiping noses

✔ Sun protection, as appropriate

✔ Diaper bag (if needed)

✔ Money for locker

✔ Bath toys

✔ Shampoo and shower items

✔ Spare socks/pants for child as these often get dropped

✔ Plastic bags for soggy stuff

✔ Bottle of milk for afterwards if child is bottle-fed

✔ Drink for older child

✔ Healthy snacks to nourish and distract afterwards

✔ Toy or bath book to amuse your child while you dress and undress

Flotation aids

There are several types of flotation aids for helping new swimmers, from simple foam boards to complete buoyancy vests. It's a good idea to see how children do in the water during early pool visits before deciding what, if any, flotation aid to use.

Safety...

Always remember that flotation aids are NEVER a substitute for close supervision. They will not stop children from drowning.

With and without

It's important that children get used to being in and around water both with and without flotation aids. This means they can experience the support and buoyancy the aids offer, while avoiding becoming overdependent on them and still recognizing that they may not yet be able to swim without support.

Choosing an aid

Whatever type of flotation aid you choose, make sure it meets the national safety standards and bears appropriate safety warnings*. Talk to other adults about their children's experiences with flotation aids, and, if appropriate, borrow one to try it out.

Look for aids that give support and allow children to lie as flat as possible in the water, but don't restrict movement too much. Babies and young children need to get used to the look and feel of an aid before they can use it effectively. These pages contain information about the most common aids.

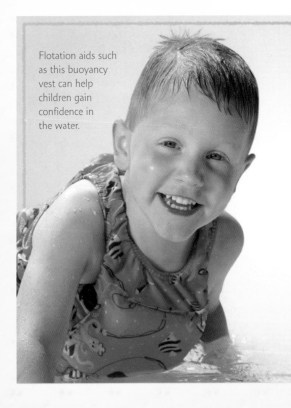

Flotation aids such as this buoyancy vest can help children gain confidence in the water.

Flotation aids: pros

✓ Build up children's confidence in the water

✓ Can give children stability while they learn swimming postures and actions

✓ Offer variety and relaxation

Flotation aids: cons

✗ Some children become reliant on them and find it difficult to make the transition to unaided swimming

✗ Can foster a false sense of security in some children

✗ Can foster a false sense of security in adults – a flotation aid isn't a life jacket, and children must still be supervised at all times

* In the US, flotation aids should meet with US Coast Guard standards and carry the following warnings: "Use only under competent supervision", "Will not protect against drowning", "To be worn on upper arm only" (for armbands).

Armbands

✓ Encourage independence in water

✗ May restrict arm movement

✗ Not suitable for babies under 12 months

These inflatable plastic cuffs keep the arms afloat while allowing the rest of the body to move freely. Make sure the armbands are small enough to stay on, and choose a style with a flat strip that sits where the arm rests against the upper body, to allow as much arm movement as possible. Styles with two inflatable chambers and safety valves are safest and have the benefit that the amount of air in the lower chamber can be reduced as children gain confidence.

Squeeze the safety valve while inflating or deflating the chamber.

Press the valve down into the inflated chamber.

Tip...

Partially inflate armbands before putting them on children's arms, then finish inflating them once they are in position. Release some of the air before you pull them off.

One advantage of double-chamber armbands like these is that if one part is punctured, the other will still offer children some support.

Armdiscs

✓ Easy to fit

✓ Versatile

✓ Less restrictive than armbands

✗ Not suitable for babies under 12 months

Armdiscs are foam discs that clip together to give variable buoyancy. Most children use three discs on each arm to start with, then gradually reduce the number as they become more confident in the water.

Flexible foam cuffs hold arm discs in place.

Inflatable rings

✗ Unsuitable for non-swimmers

Inflatable rings (rubber rings) are not recommended as flotation aids for non-swimmers. Babies and very young children can fall out of them and, when used with armbands, they can lift a child's body so high out of the water that they lose the ability to balance. Inflatable rings can be fun to play with for older children who can swim.

Baby seats

✓ Allow babies to kick freely

✗ Weight restrictions apply (refer to manufacturers' guidelines)

✗ Can tip easily

Baby seats like this are safer than rubber rings, but you must still stay close at hand as they can easily topple over.

Floating baby seats are inflatable cushions with a sunken seating pouch that has holes for babies' legs to dangle through. They are suitable for babies who can sit, but who are no more than a certain weight (for example 25lbs (11.5kg)) for each size of seat. They allow babies to splash and kick freely, but they should only be used for a short time, as babies soon get chilly with their shoulders out of the water.

Buoyancy clothing

✓ Many styles to choose from

✓ Some styles allow independence to be built up gradually

✗ Not suitable for babies under 12 months

Buoyancy clothing includes belts, backpack-style harnesses, vests, jackets and bathing suits with built-in or removable foam floats. Styles with removable floats allow children to gain independence gradually.

Buoyancy belt

Floats

✓ Can be used for 12 months and up

✓ Useful for leg and arm action practice

✗ It is easy for children to let go of them inadvertently

Polystyrene floats are useful for encouraging a horizontal position in the water. There are various types: the most common are flat floats sometimes known as kickboards. You may be able to start using floats with children as young as one year old, unless they are teething, when they tend to bite pieces out of them, which could cause them to choke.

Pull-buoys are shaped floats, usually used by advanced swimmers, that are held between the legs or ankles for support.

These children are using flat floats called kickboards to keep their bodies horizontal while they practice kicking.

Noodles

✓ Versatile

✓ Allow children to experiment
   with balance in the water

✓ Allow arms and legs to move freely

✗ Not suitable for babies who are teething

Children can use noodles to support them while they are on their front, as shown here, or on their back.

These long,
flexible foam tubes
can be used from an
early age to support the upper
body, tummy, back or legs. As with
flat floats, close supervision is needed
because children can let go of noodles and
may sink. They can also be used in conjunction
with other aids, such as armbands or armdiscs.

Specialized supports

Various specialized supports are available for
swimmers with particular physical needs. A mobility
specialist or physiotherapist should be able to advise you.

Comparison of flotation aids...

	Suitable for babies under 1 year?	Easy to reduce dependency?	Suitable for stroke practice?
Armbands	✗	✓	✓ *leg action
Armdiscs	✗	✓	✓ *leg action
Baby seats	✓ *with supervision	n/a	✗
Buoyancy clothing	✗	✓	✗
Floats	✗	✓	✓
Inflatable rings	✗	✗	✗
Noodles	✓ *with supervision	✓	✓

Going to the swimming pool

Once children are confident playing, swishing and splashing in the bathtub, they should be ready for you to take them to a swimming pool.

Early visits to the pool

The first time you take children to a pool it's a good idea just to look around and watch from the viewing area, so they can get used to the atmosphere. On your next visit you may want to get changed and go to the poolside. If they seem interested, you may decide to get in the water. Don't worry if you have to repeat this a few times.

Non-swimming adults

You don't need to be able to swim to take babies or young children swimming: you'll be in shallow water and they won't be ready to learn strokes for a while. It's important not to appear nervous of the water, though, as your fear may be transmitted to the child. If you are nervous, go with another adult who is confident, join an adult and child class, or even consider taking swimming lessons yourself.

Adult and child classes

These are usually for babies up to the age of about three to four, with an adult. They are a great way of getting you started with teaching children to swim and encouraging you to go to the pool regularly. You can find out what classes are available from pools, libraries or the local parks department.

Before you enroll, you might want to visit a class and check on the pool's facilities. Classes should be small enough for the teacher to be able to give individual advice, and must have no more than 12 babies, each with an adult. Look for classes with a relaxed, happy atmosphere, and make sure the teacher has a recognized qualification*. The atmosphere will be quieter and the water smoother if the class has exclusive use of a pool, not just one area roped off from other swimmers.

Classes like this one give adults and children the chance to learn new skills in a relaxed, informal environment, under the supervision of a qualified teacher.

*The American Red Cross and YMCAs are two qualified organizations offering lessons by certified instructors.

Swimming pool safety

Following these guidelines will help you keep children safe at the swimming pool:

- Never leave babies or young children unattended at the pool, even for a moment, in or out of the water. Don't even turn your back on them.

- Children who can't swim should be watched closely in the water and on the poolside and even those who can swim need close supervision.

- Teach children from the start that they must never:
  - run along the poolside
  - push people
  - jump in too close to them
  - splash people
  - grab hold of them
  - try to duck them

Children who are just learning to walk need very close supervision in and around the pool.

First time in the pool

Your first time in the pool is likely to be most enjoyable if you go on a day when you have plenty of time and both you and the child are in good spirits. Don't go when a child is tired or hungry, or for an hour after a meal or feeding. The main goal is for them to enjoy themselves, so don't try to do too much or stay in the pool too long. Make a mental list of the things you want to do so you don't end up just standing around.

When not to swim

It's unwise to take babies or young children swimming if they seem even slightly unwell. They shouldn't swim if they have a cold, or any nose, throat, chest, ear or eye infection; if they have diarrhea or an upset stomach; or if they have athlete's foot, which is highly contagious. Many pools allow people with verrucas to swim if these are covered with water-resistant gel or a rubber sock (both available from a pharmacy).

If children have additional medical needs, such as asthma, diabetes or epilepsy, it's a good idea to talk to their doctor or health care provider before taking them swimming for the first time.

Before...

Make sure that swimsuits and trunks are clean before you go swimming. Clean babies' bottoms before putting swim diapers on them and wipe their noses if you need to. Make sure children's hands, faces and knees are clean, and give them a shower if necessary. Get them to blow their noses and go to the bathroom. Make sure they (and you) aren't eating candy or gum – besides being unhygienic, these can be a choking hazard. Once you're in the water, respond quickly to requests to go to the bathroom. If babies show signs of going to the bathroom, get out right away.

...and after

After swimming, everyone should go in the shower to rinse off the chemicals in the water as these can irritate the skin. You don't need to use soap, though. It's important to dry children's ears, particularly after swimming. Tilt their head first to one side for a few seconds, then to the other, to let the water drain out. Then dry them with a towel. Bring a towel or bathrobe to wrap around yourself while you are getting children dressed. By the time you've finished dressing them, you'll almost be dry yourself.

How long to stay in

Remember to note the time you get in, and don't extend the maximum times given here. If the water is too warm or too cold, then these times should be reduced.

Age of child	0–6 months	6–18 months	18 months –3 years	3 years and older
Maximum on 1st visit	10 minutes	15 minutes	20 minutes	30 minutes
Maximum after several visits	30 minutes	30 minutes	40 minutes	45 minutes (no more than 30 to be spent working hard)

Length of time in the pool

This depends on the water temperature, the age of the children, and how much fun they're having. The chart above shows the maximum time children should spend in the pool. It's important to build up to these times slowly. Even if children are happy, they may get chilled or overtired. If they're cold and shivering, get them out right away. Wrap them in a towel at once, then dry and dress them before you get changed yourself. Dress them extra warmly to go out in cool weather, and make sure they wear a hat.

Nervous children

Some children may refuse to get into the pool at first. This is quite a common response, as to a child, this water can be more frightening than the bathtub at home. Avoid forcing them in; just let them watch from the poolside or walk around pointing out how much fun other children are having. Encourage them to sit on the edge and dangle their feet in the water with you.

If this happens for several visits, it may be worth trying to get in the water anyway. If children are still very scared, it may be better to give up the idea of swimming for a few months, then try again.

Using flotation aids

The advantages and disadvantages of using flotation aids are discussed in detail on pages 18–21. Whatever you decide, it's important to use aids as and when appropriate and to avoid overusing them. It's much better for children's confidence if they get used to entering and leaving the water without them.

You can often help put nervous children at ease by holding them close and establishing eye contact as soon as you can.

Getting into the water

The ideal way to get into the pool with a baby is to give the baby to someone else to hold while you get in, then have them pass the baby to you. If there's no one else available, you can try these ways, depending on the age of the baby.

Safety...

Always bring children back to the side after entering the pool and encourage them to hold on to the wall or gutter. This is important for safety as it conditions them always to make for the edge after jumping or falling into the water.

Poolside entry

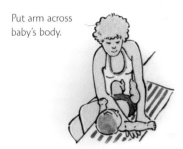

Put arm across baby's body.

Lay the baby on a towel or mat by the pool. Sit down, keeping hold of the baby with one hand.

Slide in backward.

With one arm across the baby's body to stop them from rolling, turn and slide into the water.

Lift baby in.

When your feet are firmly on the bottom of the pool, lift the baby in to join you.

Protect child with arm as you slide in.

With babies who can sit up or young children, slide in as shown here, putting one arm across the child.

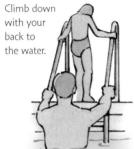

Climb down with your back to the water.

With young children who can manage the ladder, go down first, then help them down the same way.

Child turns backward and slides in.

At the age of about 18 months, you can encourage children to turn and slide backward into the water.

Be careful not to bang chin on poolside.

Get in yourself first, so you can help them, especially if they're too small to touch the bottom.

Shallow steps or a slope

With babies, just walk straight into the pool, holding them securely. You will be top-heavy carrying a child, so slide your feet along the bottom to avoid slipping.

Let toddlers and older children walk in, holding your hand and sliding their feet along the bottom. As they gain confidence over the sessions you can encourage them to walk in without holding hands.

Hold baby securely.

Slide feet along bottom.

Jumping in

This is a great confidence-builder, which you can start teaching even young babies, once they've been to the pool a few times and are happy in the water.

Start by sitting babies on the edge of the pool. At about a year you can stand them on the edge, but continue to hold them under their shoulders, not by the hands, or there'll be too much pressure on their shoulder joints.

Holding the child under their shoulders, lift them into the water, so that it comes up to their shoulders. To make it more fun, you can sing *Humpty Dumpty* while you do this.

As soon as they are in the water, turn them onto their front and glide them back to the side of the pool, showing them how to hold on to the wall or gutter.

When they're used to being lifted in and provided they know how to blow out in the water, you can start momentarily submerging them after lifting them in.

Jumping in alone

Gradually, you'll be able to encourage children to jump in to you on their own. The water needs to be at least 3 feet (0.9m) deep for this to be safe. To begin with, catch them under their arms before they go under.

Teach them to position their toes over the edge before jumping, and to jump well out from the wall to avoid hitting it; never let them run and jump into the water as they may slip and hurt themselves. Encourage them to bend their knees after entering the water. Always glide them back to the wall after they jump, until they can swim back on their own.

It's important that you're ready to catch children when they first start to jump in like this. Give them a cue such as "One, two, three, jump!", get them to join in and later give the cue themselves.

Holding children

There are various ways to support children in the water. What you choose will depend on the amount of independent control they have of their head and posture, and how much support they need for an activity. Here are some of the commonly used holds. Positions for particular activities are described later with the activities.

Cradle hold

This hold is particularly suitable for babies who can't yet support their head. It allows you to talk to them easily and to maintain eye contact. Being held close will help them to feel safe.

Keep a baby's ears out of the water to start with.

Protective hold

With the baby's back to your chest, hold them with one hand across the chest, and the thumb supporting the chin. Use your other hand to support their thighs until you're deep enough for the water's buoyancy to hold them up. This hold is useful for moving babies through the water or passing them to another adult.

You can use this hold with babies starting at the age of two months.

Remember...

Hold children gently and confidently, but also allow them to experience the support offered by the water.

Carry hold

With the baby in a seated position, bring one arm around their back and hold the leg furthest away from you. Use your other hand to support their back and shoulder. Their near arm should be over your shoulder and their head close to yours, so you can make good eye contact, smile and talk to them.

Use this hold with children who can control their head but can't yet sit.

Hip hold

As children grow and their posture control develops, you'll be able to sit them on your hip, with one leg on either side of you. Like the carry hold, this position is useful for entering the water where the pool has a sloping entry, and for moving around in it.

Put one arm around the child's back and the other hand underneath for support.

First activities

First activities in the water should aim to get children to relax, enjoy themselves and build their confidence. Here are some ideas for things you could try at the start of each session. Singing songs and nursery rhymes can be useful for helping children relax too.

Face to face

It helps give children confidence if you always keep your face on a level with theirs. With a baby or toddler, this may mean kneeling on the pool bottom, if it's shallow enough. In deeper water, you'll probably feel more stable and comfortable standing with your legs wide apart and knees slightly bent.

How much to do

The activities on these two pages may be enough for a baby or nervous child's first visit. With an older toddler or child who takes to the water easily, you may want to go on to the activities described on the following pages.

Standing on the bottom

Depending on the depth of the water, children may not be tall enough to stand on the bottom of the pool right away. This means that unless there's a gently sloping entrance they can't do the walking, running and jumping activities described opposite to begin with. If children can touch the bottom on their first visit, encourage them to stand from the start.

Sprinkling toys like this one can help babies become more familiar with the feeling of water trickling onto their skin.

Sinking and bobbing

Stay in one place to start with, then walk slowly around the pool.

Hold the child close. (Hold a child who is standing by the hands.)

Gently sink down until your shoulders are in the water.

Rise and sink again, so the child gets used to the lapping water.

Bouncing

If children are happy, start bouncing gently up and down, holding them close to you, then farther away as their confidence increases. Try singing action songs such as *Pop! goes the weasel* as you bounce.

Hold the child in front of you.

Lift them up gently.

Lower them with a gentle splash.

Trickling water

When children are used to water on their body, gently trickle some over the back of their head, then, if they like it, try a few drops over their face. You could sing one of the trickling water songs shown on page 31.

Blowing bubbles

If they are happy putting their mouths in the water, encourage children to blow bubbles. This is the first stage of learning to breathe correctly when swimming, so it's a useful skill as well as being fun.

Water play

Take along one or two favorite bath toys and see if the baby will pat them along. Older babies and toddlers might like to "wash" themselves with a sponge or pour water over themselves from a container.

Walk, run and jump

If children are tall enough to stand, get them to walk across the pool holding your hand, or slide their feet along the bottom. They could then try running across, or pretending to be a kangaroo and jumping across.

Action songs

Action songs are great for encouraging children to do things in the water that they might otherwise be reluctant to do, such as getting their face wet. They often play a large part in adult and child swimming classes, too.

Some action songs, such as the *Hokey pokey*, work particularly well with mixed-age groups like this one.

Using action songs

On these pages the actions are shown in italic type and ideas for extra verses are marked with asterisks (*). Unless you're carrying the child, stay where the water is shallow enough for them to stand on the bottom of the pool.

Ring around the rosie

(Hold hands and walk around in a circle.)
Ring around the rosie,
A pocket full of posies,
Ashes. ashes,
We all fall down!
(Crouch down or briefly duck under water.)

(Circle again, crouching low in the water.)
The cows are in the meadow,
Eating buttercups,
(Blow bubbles into the water.)
Ashes. ashes,
We all jump up!
(Jump high out of the water.)

Oh, the grand old Duke of York

(March in one spot, or bounce baby gently up and down in time. Hold the baby facing you to start with, then later with their back toward you.)
Oh, the grand old Duke of York,
He had ten thousand men:
He marched them up to the top of the hill,
(Walk forward or lift baby up.)
And he marched them down again.
(Walk backward or bring baby down.)
And when they were up they were up,
(Walk forward or lift baby up.)
And when they were down they were down,
(Walk backward or bring baby down.)
And when they were only halfway up,
(One step forward or lift baby up a little.)
They were neither up nor down.
(One step backward or lift baby right up then down.)

This one is also good for exercising adults' arms.

Round the mulberry bush

(Hold hands and walk around in a circle.)
Here we go round the mulberry bush,
The mulberry bush, the mulberry bush,
Here we go round the mulberry bush
On a cold and frosty morning.
This is the way we *jump up and down**,
Jump up and down, jump up and down,
This is the way we *jump up and down*,
On a cold and frosty morning.

**Kick our legs, turn around, wash our face,
take a shower, wash our hair, blow bubbles*

Hokey pokey

(Stand in a circle.)
You put your *right foot in*.
You put your *right foot out*.
You put your *right foot in*,
And you *splash it all about*.
You do the hokey pokey,
And you turn yourself about. *(Turn in a circle.)*
That's what it's all about! *(Clap hands.)*

You put your *left foot** *in*.
You put your *left foot out*.
You put your *left foot in*,
And you *splash it all about*.
You do the hokey pokey,
And you turn yourself about. *(Turn in a circle.)*
That's what it's all about! *(Clap hands.)*

**Right hand, left hand, whole face, whole self*

If you're happy and you know it

If you're happy and you know it,
Splash your hands*;
If you're happy and you know it,
Splash your hands;
If you're happy and you know it,
And you really want to show it;
If you're happy and you know it,
Splash your hands.

**Kick your legs, turn around, wash your
face, take a shower, wash your hair,
blow bubbles*

Trickling water songs

Sprinkle water with your fingers at first. As children gain confidence, you can use your hands, then toys or cups to sprinkle and pour. The carry hold is described on page 27.

Mary, Mary, quite contrary

(Carry hold, sprinkle water over child.)
Mary, Mary, quite contrary,
How does your garden grow?
With silver bells and cockle shells,
And pretty maids all in a row.

Doctor Foster

(Carry hold, sprinkle water over child.)
Doctor Foster went to Gloucester
In a shower of rain.
He stepped in a puddle
(Sink lower in water.)
Right up to his middle
And never went there again.

Itsy Bitsy spider

*(Carry hold, with your shoulders in
the water, and gradually stand up.)*
The itsy bitsy spider
Crawled up the water spout;
Down came the rain
(Trickle water on baby.)
And washed the spider out.
(Swish baby from side to side.)
Out came the sun
And dried up all the rain,
(Blow on baby's face.)
And the itsy bitsy spider
Crawled up the spout again.
(Sink down and gradually stand up again.)

*Repeat the song
and actions in
different styles, for
example as a slow
or tiny spider.*

Bouncing and jumping songs

Bounce children up and down in time with the rhyme of these songs. Start with gentle splashes and make bigger lifts and splashes where indicated.

Humpty Dumpty

Humpty Dumpty sat on a wall,
Humpty Dumpty had a great fall;
(Lift up and splash down.)
All the King's horses, and all the King's men
Couldn't put Humpty together again.
(Lift up and splash down.)

(To use this song to get children into the pool, start with them sitting on the poolside and lift them in at "had a great fall.")

Hickory, dickory, dock

Hickory, dickory, dock!
(Lift up and splash down.)
The mouse ran up the clock;
(Lift and hold.)
The clock struck one,
(Say "Bong!")
The mouse ran down,
(Splash down.)
Hickory, dickory, dock!

Tip...

Older children can have fun adapting the rhymes and making up actions of their own.

Pop! goes the weasel

Half a pound of tuppenny rice,
Half a pound of treacle.
That's the way the money goes,
Pop! goes the weasel.
(Lift up and splash down.)
Up and down the City Road,
In and out The Eagle,
That's the way the money goes,
Pop! goes the weasel.
(Lift up and splash down.)

Floating songs

Children can float with or without a flotation aid or adult support, lying on their front or their back.

Twinkle, twinkle

Twinkle, twinkle, little star,
How I wonder what you are.
Up above the world so high,
Like a diamond in the sky;
Twinkle, twinkle, little star,
How I wonder what you are.

It's important to maintain good eye contact with children during action songs, and encourage them with lots of smiles and hugs.

Rocking and swishing songs

You can use these gentle songs with young babies from the beginning. Older children can use them to practice floating on their front and back, spreading their arms and legs out into star shapes, or curling up into a tuck position, then stretching straight again in time to the music.

Rock-a-bye baby

(Cradle hold (see page 27), rock baby from side to side.)
>Rock-a-bye baby, on the tree top,
>When the wind blows, the cradle will rock;
>When the bough breaks, the cradle will fall,
>And down will come baby, cradle and all.

Bring back my bonnie

(Hold child on their front and swish them gently from side to side.)
>My bonnie lies over the ocean,
>My bonnie lies over the sea;
>My bonnie lies over the ocean,
>Oh, bring back my bonnie to me.

(Hold child out in front and whoosh toward you on each "bring back.")
>Bring back, bring back,
>Bring back my bonnie to me, to me;
>Bring back, bring back,
>Bring back my bonnie to me.

(End with a big hug.)

Rolling and turning over songs

Young children will need you to roll and turn them over (see page 37) but older children will be able to practice rolling over and turning themselves.

There were ten in the bed

>There were ten* in the bed
>And the little one said,
>"*Roll over, roll over;*"
>So they all *rolled over*
>And one fell out.

Nine, eight, seven ... one
('And the little one said "Good night!"')

Teddy Bear, Teddy Bear

>Teddy Bear, Teddy Bear, *turn around,*
>Teddy Bear, Teddy Bear, *touch the ground,*
>Teddy Bear, Teddy Bear, *reach up high,*
>Teddy Bear, Teddy Bear, *wink one eye,*
>Teddy Bear, Teddy Bear, *slap your knees,*
>Teddy Bear, Teddy Bear, *sit down please.*

I'm a little pancake

Sing to the tune of I'm a little teapot.

(Start with child floating on back, swish them gently from side to side.)

>I'm a little pancake on my back.
>I'm a little pancake, nice and flat.
>When I'm nearly ready, cooked and browned,
>Flip me over, *(Turn child onto front.)*
>Turn me around.

>I'm a little pancake, upside down.
>I'm a little pancake, golden brown.
>When I smell delicious, nearly done,
>Flip me over, *(Turn child over.)*
>Yum, yum, yum!

Hold the child under the arms to turn them over.

Getting afloat

As soon as children are happy in the water you can start thinking about getting them afloat. Some children are confident enough to get into a horizontal position on their very first visit to the pool, but most prefer to remain upright for the first few sessions.

Planning a session

Start each session with introductory activities from the previous section, then progress to the activities described here. Avoid rushing through activities, and remember that children feel more confident if you keep down to their level, maintain eye contact, smile and talk reassuringly.

Supporting children in water

There are various ways of supporting children in the water, that are appropriate at different stages of their development. All the positions shown on these pages can also be used to encourage a kicking action. With babies and young children, remember to use the "Kick, kick!" cue.

Supporting young babies

Young babies without much control of their head need help to keep their face out of the water. Hold them under their arms, with your wrists together to support their chin, then move backward, telling them to kick.

Put your thumbs over the child's shoulders.

As they gain strength in their neck, support them under their arms only. Keep them low in the water so they can feel its buoyancy, not just your support. Their chin should rest on the surface of the water.

Some children may dislike water on their upper body early on, but you can gradually lower them and yourself into the water as they get more used to the sensation.

Supporting from the side

As children gain confidence in the water, you can support them from the side, with your hands around their upper chest, and your thumbs around their shoulders. Hold them gently and firmly to start with, and relax your grip a little when they're ready.

It's difficult to maintain eye contact in this position, so keep talking to reassure the child.

Supporting toddlers

At about two years old, as children gain strength and confidence, you can reduce your support and hold them gently by their upper arms, then their forearms and then their hands.

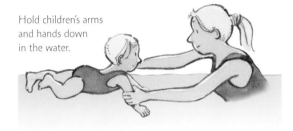

Hold children's arms and hands down in the water.

Using the side

Encourage children to hold the side or gutter at the pool edge while lifting their legs up. You may need to put your hand under their tummy at first. Encourage them to relax.

Children will stretch out in a flatter position as they gain confidence.

Using floats

At about eighteen months, you can give children a float to hold under each arm. Be prepared to give extra support by holding their floats and walking backward. Make sure they don't let go.

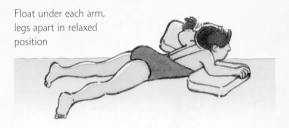

Float under each arm, legs apart in relaxed position

Using a noodle

Give children a noodle to hold in front of them with both hands, while resting their chin on the foam bar and lifting their legs. To start with, some children may need support under their armpits as you walk backward through the water.

Chin resting on noodle

When they have gained confidence, get them to lean forward onto a noodle and tuck it under their arms, lifting their legs and letting the noodle and the water take their weight. Again, you may need to give extra support under the armpits initially, or to hold their hands to encourage them to lean forward.

Noodle supporting child under armpits

Support on the back

Most young babies respond best to being put on their back in the water. Support them under their head and bottom then, once they seem secure, gently take your hand from under their bottom. They will probably float quite happily. Some young babies can even float for a few moments without any support at all, but have your hands ready to take over again. Gently move the child sideways, supporting them with one or both hands.

Help babies lie flat in the water by waving, or holding a toy above them.

Supporting an older baby

Babies who can sit up often object to being put on their back in the water. To help them feel more secure, let them rest their head on your shoulder, with their face against your cheeks and their ears out of the water. Hold them under their arms or, for greater security, stretch your arms out underneath their body and hold their legs.

Rest the child's head on your shoulder and hold their arms or legs.

If you want to initiate a kick, hold a baby's legs below the knee, and gently move their legs in a kicking action, as you walk backward through the water, repeating the cue, "Kick, kick!"

Supporting older children

Get toddlers or older children to lie back in the water while you stand behind them and support them under their arms. Encourage them to relax and enjoy the floating sensation.

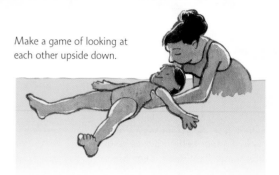

Make a game of looking at each other upside down.

Using floats

At about 18 months, see if children will lie back and float, holding a float under each arm. Give them extra support under their shoulders at first, if they want it, and make sure they hold the floats firmly.

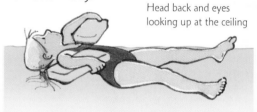

Head back and eyes looking up at the ceiling

Using a noodle

Give children a noodle and let them tuck it under their arms and lean backward onto it, lifting their legs and feeling the buoyancy offered by the noodle and the water. They may need you to support under their back to start with.

Legs relaxed in a comfortable position

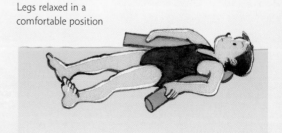

Turning over in the water

This is a good confidence-building skill and can be useful if children are not especially happy in a certain position. To turn the child over again, roll them back the way they came.

Keep young babies' mouths clear of the water.

Hold the child under their arms, standing at the side if they're on their front, or behind if they're on their back. Gently roll them over.

They may like to pretend to be a pancake in a pan and sing *I'm a little pancake*. Roll them over at the words "flip me over."

You could also sing *There were ten in the bed*, rolling them over on "roll over." Eventually, they'll learn to turn themselves over.

Kicking

Most babies and young children kick spontaneously in the water but if they don't, try making their legs kick to give them the idea. Rest the top of their body against your chest and shoulder, then stretch your arms under their tummy if they're on their front, or their bottom if they're on their back. Hold their legs below the knee and move them up and down, repeating the kicking cue as you walk backward across the pool.

Hold children's legs below the knee, keeping the kick under the water.

Encourage children to keep their legs straight as they lie back in the water and kick.

Kicking using a float

At about eighteen months, children can practice kicking while lying on their front or back, with a float under each arm. Give them extra support by holding them under the shoulders until you

feel they're completely comfortable. Alternatively you may have to hold their hands on the floats so they keep a good grip. Let them hold the floats on their own when they're ready.

Hold your hands over the child's on the float to start with.

Be ready to support their shoulders or head if needed.

The next stage is to hold a single float between you and the child, and walk backward, guiding them as they kick.

Give children a single float to hug to their chest as they lie on their back and kick. Walk backward as they move.

Putting their feet back down

To help them stay safe, children need to learn to regain a standing position, both in shallow water (to stand up) and in deep water (to change from their front to their back, change direction or

perform another skill such as treading water). Some children can do this naturally, others may need to be taught it. This skill should be practiced using flotation aids at first.

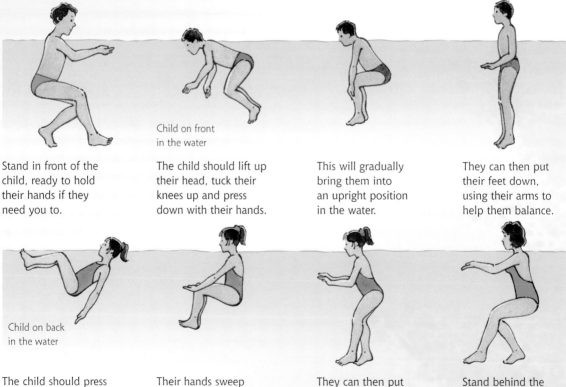

Child on front in the water

Stand in front of the child, ready to hold their hands if they need you to.

The child should lift up their head, tuck their knees up and press down with their hands.

This will gradually bring them into an upright position in the water.

They can then put their feet down, using their arms to help them balance.

Child on back in the water

The child should press down with their hands, lift up their head and tuck their knees up.

Their hands sweep forward and up, palms facing up, as they become upright.

They can then put their feet down, using their arms to help them balance.

Stand behind the child, ready to support their shoulders if needed.

Encouraging arm movement

The best way to encourage babies to move their arms is to put a toy in front of them and get them to stretch out for it. Hold them under their arms, with your fingers stretched out to support their chin if they need help supporting their head. Hold them close to you, cheek to cheek, until they gain confidence.

Keep babies low in the water so they can feel its buoyancy.

Encourage children to use their arms and legs while you continue supporting them. When you feel they are ready, gently let go, but be prepared to take hold again quickly and calmly if needed.

If children are using a flotation aid that leaves their arms free to move (for example a buoyancy vest), suggest that they use a paddling action to pull themselves toward the toy.

Early arm actions

At about nine months old, you can sit the baby on a shallow pool step or on your knee with their back to your chest, and move their hands in a "dog paddle" action so they get the idea of reaching and pulling. Remember to keep their hands in the water.

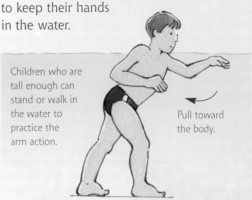

Children who are tall enough can stand or walk in the water to practice the arm action.

Pull toward the body.

You could also demonstrate other types of arm actions too, for example breast stroke arm action, and get children to copy. They can do this with and without a flotation aid or support from an adult.

Throw a bath toy a little way ahead of a child then encourage them to use their arms and legs to move through the water to grab it.

Pushing and gliding

Pushing and gliding through the water is a useful skill as it encourages the horizontal, streamlined body position which is needed for swimming efficient strokes. It also allows even young children the freedom of moving through the water unaided for a few seconds.

Keep low down, with child's chin on water.

Between two people

You can push and glide babies and children of all ages from the time they can hold their head up. Avoid forcing them to do it if they aren't enjoying it. Remember to keep down to their level, smile and let them know that something is about to happen, by giving a cue such as "Ready, set, go!"

Supporting the baby or child under the arms, one person glides them smoothly to another, who is standing a few paces away ready to take them gently again under the arms. Keep low down, with the child's chin on the water, and don't actually let go at this stage.

Keep hold of the child during glide to begin with.

Once children have grasped the idea of blowing out into the water, encourage them to put their faces in the water during the glide, if they're not doing it already.

The next stage is to let go of them for a moment just before the change-over. As they get older and their leg and arm movements get stronger, you can gradually increase the length of time you let go for and the distance between the two adults, so that the child "swims" between you.

From the side

Children may be able to start pushing and gliding from the side around the age of two. They should hold the side or gutter with both hands, put their feet on the wall and then push off and glide toward you.

Children will probably want you to catch them right away to begin with. As they gain confidence, you can gradually increase the distance you stand from the side.

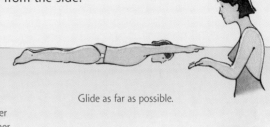

Get ready to push off with feet.

Stretch out. Bring arms together under the water and squeeze legs together.

Glide as far as possible.

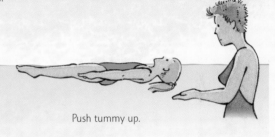

Get ready to push off with feet.

Look up.

Push tummy up.

Pushing and gliding children between two people like this can give them an early experience of "swimming" through the water.

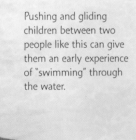
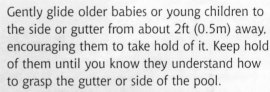

To the side

Gently glide older babies or young children to the side or gutter from about 2ft (0.5m) away, encouraging them to take hold of it. Keep hold of them until you know they understand how to grasp the gutter or side of the pool.

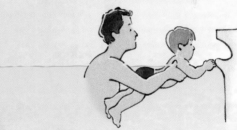

When children are tall enough, they can push off from the pool bottom and glide to the side. Encourage them to stretch out like arrows, put their face in the water and increase the distance they glide. As they push off from farther away, get them to kick their legs.

Breathing

Learning how to breathe (that is, breathing out when the face is in the water, and breathing in when the face is out of the water) is an essential part of learning to swim. Don't press children to put their face in the water in the early sessions; just encourage them if they do so spontaneously.

Blowing bubbles

The best way of learning how to breathe out is by blowing bubbles. Children learn quickly by copying, so to get started, first blow gently in the child's face to show them what to do. Get them to copy you, perhaps by pretending to blow out birthday candles. Then blow again, with your mouth on the surface of the water.

As children gain confidence, you can have fun experimenting. Vary the speed with which you blow out, to create streams of small popping bubbles, or big, loud ones. Try humming while you blow bubbles, or pretending to be speedboats or engines. If children are reluctant to blow bubbles in the pool, cup a little water in your hand and show them how to blow bubbles into it, or try blowing through a drinking straw.

Lower your hand to the water's surface as you blow.

Try to make long streams of bubbles as you blow through straws.

Get children to copy you blowing bubbles in the water.

Blowing plastic toys along the surface can help children control their breathing. Teaching aids called "egg-flips" are often used in lessons. As children blow on the "eggs," they flip over to reveal a contrasting color.

Blowing bubbles under water

Once children can blow bubbles on the surface, get them to go under doing the same thing. Gently sink down together just under the surface, then come straight up again. If they splutter, reassure them and tell them how well they've done.

Don't insist on submerging if they really hate it. It's best to do it only once or twice each session in any case. Older children who are apprehensive about putting their face in the water may be willing to do it little by little, mouth first, then nose, and so on.

Head-butt float

Older children could try moving through the water blowing bubbles while pushing a float or ball along with their nose or head. Remind them to come up to take a breath when they need to.

Blow out steadily and try to increase the length of time a breath lasts.

Motor boats

Encourage children to blow bubbles with their face in the water by getting them to push and glide and make engine noises. They can do this between two adults, or on their own with a float.

Encourage children to kick to travel farther.

Shallow water method

Learning to swim in shallow water can give children a lot of confidence. The water needs to be no deeper than 12–18 inches (30–45cm), so they can support themselves in a horizontal position with their hands on the bottom of the pool and their head out of the water. A wading pool, ocean* or lake can be an ideal place to learn to swim in this way.

Lying on front, hands on bottom of ocean or pool, head out of water

Lying on back, hands on bottom of ocean or pool, face out of water

The idea is that children walk their hands along the bottom while kicking their legs. As they become more confident, they can begin to take their hands off the bottom too and add an arm action, but with the knowledge that they can quickly put their hands back down if they need to.

Deep water method

Another approach is to teach children to swim while they're out of their depth, first with close fitting flotation aids, such as armbands, then gradually without. This method, which needs particularly close supervision, may help them gain confidence in deep water, but you need to make sure they don't become either more fearful, or overconfident.

* Extra care should be taken using this method in oceans and lakes: the seabed may drop away suddenly, and there may be strong currents.

Playing underwater games such as tag, and catching sinking objects like this dive stick are fun ways to encourage children to open their eyes under water.

Going under

Children should be introduced gradually to submersion, starting by trickling water over their body, head then face. Routinely submerging young babies is not recommended (see "Submerging young babies," opposite) and it isn't necessary as humans don't normally swim under water but along the surface. For toddlers and young children, brief submersion after jumping in, or to pick up objects from the bottom of the pool is acceptable. Avoid forcing children to submerge if they don't like it, and always be ready to help them to the surface if needed.

Here are some ideas for activities to build up children's confidence under water.

Submerging together

Hold the child close, facing you. Give the cue "Ready, go!" or "1, 2, 3" then blow on their face and bend your knees so you're both submerged briefly. By blowing on them you'll encourage them to hold their breath. It's important that you smile, and remember to praise them when you come up. If they splutter, reassure them. Only do this once or twice in any session, and only repeat it if the child seems happy.

Blow on child's face then submerge together.

Sinking action songs

There are several action songs that provide contexts for brief submersions. With young children you could try singing *Ring around the rosie*, briefly submerging them at the words "We all fall down." *Oranges and lemons* gives a good opportunity for older children to duck briefly under the water as they go under the arch, and *See-saw, Margery Daw* is an ideal accompaniment for them to bob in and out of the water.

Two adults or older children hold hands to make an arch for *Oranges and lemons*.

Encourage children to open their eyes under water by asking if they can see you when you submerge together.

Sunken toys

Sit babies or toddlers on a step or in a very shallow part of the pool next to a sunken toy and get them to reach and pick it up. Support them in a sitting position and don't let them swallow the water.

Hold a toy or ring under water for older children to retrieve, gradually holding it lower in the water as they become more confident. In shallow water, you can allow the toy to sink to the bottom of the pool. Many stores sell weighted rings and sticks that are designed to sink slowly. Children can either wait until these have sunk to the bottom of the pool, or try to intercept them before they reach there.

Submerging young babies

A few methods of teaching advocate frequent or deep submersion. Opinion is divided, but some experts say these are best avoided for various reasons.

- Going too deep in the water can put a dangerous amount of pressure on a young child's ears. The pressure on a baby's ears at a depth of 3 feet (1m) is equivalent to that of an adult at 16 feet (5m) – a deep diving pit.

- Frequent submerging may increase the risk of ear infections.

- It can be dangerous for children to swallow a very large amount of water.

- Frequent submerging may have long-term psychological effects that are not immediately apparent.

Children who swim under water

Children who swim unaided before the age of about three will do so just under the surface. Don't discourage them, but watch them very closely and help them to come to the surface for air. Signs of needing to take a breath include shaking their heads or moving their arms and legs faster. Guide them to the surface right away, holding them under their arms or chin. Eventually they'll learn to surface on their own.

Some babies naturally swim under water like this, but you need to make sure they come up for a breath.

Progressing to strokes

It is important not to try to rush children through the stages of learning to swim or to start teaching them to do the proper strokes (front crawl, back crawl and breast stroke) too soon. Always remember that your main goal is for children to enjoy the water.

Children don't have the strength to swim on the surface of the water until they're about three. Then, they may be able to do a dog paddle type of stroke on their front, and swim on their back with their arms by their sides.

Remember...

Children's progress in swimming may vary considerably. Although you may feel a child is learning slowly, providing they continue to enjoy their experiences in the water, they too will swim competently in time.

When to start

Before children start to learn the major strokes, they should be able to swim at least 10 yards (about 9m) on their own and be happy doing all the activities described so far in the book. Some children may be able to start the strokes as early as age four or five, though it's unusual for children to have the strength or understanding to do them properly before they're six or seven. At the same time as children start learning the strokes, they can be introduced to other water skills as well.

Children need to have the strokes and skills demonstrated to them. If you aren't a good swimmer yourself, find someone else they can watch, and go through the pictures in this book with them. You may also want to start thinking about classes. Many pools hold classes for children without their caregivers starting at the age of three, though some children may prefer to stay in adult and child classes until they are four. You can find out what classes are available from the pools, the library or local parks department.

The building blocks

To swim successfully, children need to combine the ability to float with a means of propeling themselves through the water. It's important to build up each stroke gradually and systematically, first teaching the body position, then the legs, arms, breathing and finally the timing and coordination.

Planning a session

Once you start teaching children the strokes, remember that swimming should always be fun. Continue to start the session with introductory activities of the type shown earlier in the book. Spend about a third of the session on a stroke and, following that, add a contrasting skill. Make sure you leave enough time for them to play in the water at the end of the session.

Here is one possible way of breaking up the time in a 30-minute session:

- 1 minute
  Discuss with the child what you are going to do in the session.

- 4 minutes
  Do some introductory activities and/or swim a stroke the child already knows, say front crawl.

- 12 minutes
  Learn a new stroke, say back crawl.

- 8 minutes
  Introduce a contrasting water skill, say treading water, and practice previously learned strokes and skills.

- 5 minutes
  Play time. Let children do what they like but remember to watch them closely and give help when it's needed.

Specific needs

All children develop confidence and skill in water at different rates, so it's important always to allow children to learn at their own pace. In addition, some children may have other specific needs to consider when you're planning a session at the swimming pool.

Getting advice

There are relatively few long-term medical conditions that make it inadvisable to take children to a swimming pool, and there are many benefits to be gained from taking part in appropriate activity in the water. These range from physical benefits such as toned muscles, increased stamina and improved coordination, to opportunities for developing social skills and self-confidence as well as having lots of fun.

If you're thinking about taking a child with specific needs to the swimming pool, it's a good idea to gather as much information as you can. Consult your family doctor or other members of your child's healthcare team and, if you can, learn from the experiences of other parents and caregivers, through support groups or national organizations. Their advice, combined with your own knowledge of the child, will enable you to decide how best the child's needs can be met.

Learning together

Some pools offer separate sessions for people with specific needs in addition to regular pool access. As with other aspects of children's development, it's important to emphasize the similarities with other children, rather than the differences. Your positive approach will help them to achieve their potential, and you'll both learn along the way when adjustments need to be made, and what these should be. Set realistic goals and be proud of their achievements.

The information on the following pages addresses some of the practical issues you may need to consider. You can also visit the Usborne Quicklinks website at **www.usborne-quicklinks.com** for links to organizations which may give you further guidance.

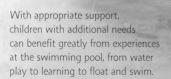

With appropriate support, children with additional needs can benefit greatly from experiences at the swimming pool, from water play to learning to float and swim.

Asthma

Swimming is usually an excellent form of exercise for children and young people with asthma. The warm humid air in the pool is less likely to trigger symptoms of asthma. However, this is not the case for everyone and swimming in cold or chlorinated water can trigger some people's asthma. If swimming does make a child's asthma worse, always ensure they use their rescue inhaler immediately before they swim, and have it close by when they swim, in case they need it.

Autistic spectrum disorders

Take children to the pool at a time when it's quiet, and there are as few distractions as possible. Wearing ear plugs and plastic sunglasses can help to reduce the amount of aural and visual stimulation at the pool. Alternatively, playing gentle music can help to camouflage sounds too.

Highly structured sessions can give children a reassuring routine and then you can introduce new skills gradually within a familiar framework. Children might find it reassuring if you identify a spot at the side of the pool that they can return to after each activity. You may find it effective to use equipment of the same type, texture and color to work on the same skills, for example always to practice front-crawl leg action with a blue, smooth float. Using laminated task cards to introduce particular activities, such as taking a shower, can also help to relay information and reinforce ideas.

Babies with Down's syndrome often take very well to the water and go on to become confident swimmers.

Continence management

A child's care team will be able to advise on how best to manage continence in the pool. Successful control can often be achieved by combining specialized swimwear or appliances with their usual continence management techniques.

Diabetes

If children have Type 1 diabetes, it is important to check their blood glucose levels before and after exercise. Swimming can use a lot of energy so make sure they eat extra carbohydrates (such as crackers or fruit) before going in the pool, and after the session too. Take along a plastic container of dilute sugary drink, in case their blood glucose levels drop too low during the session. If they start to show symptoms of a hypo, get them out of the pool and give them a sugary drink followed by a carbohydrate snack.

Down's syndrome

It's especially important to maintain good eye contact while giving instructions. Repetition and review will help reinforce activities and skills you have practiced together, and it's important to set clear expectations and limits. Some activities, such as diving, may be unsuitable for children who have cervical spine instability, so check with the child's specialist.

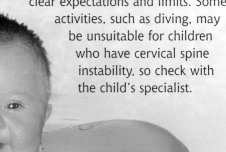

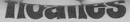

Epilepsy

Children with epilepsy should never swim alone or take unnecessary risks. If there is a lifeguard present, make them aware of the child's epilepsy. A "buddy system" is a discreet way of supervising swimmers, especially as they get older. The buddy will swim with them and be able to offer help. If no qualified lifeguard is present, the child should not swim deeper than the buddy's shoulder height. If a buddy system can't be used, it may be better for a "supervisor" to watch from the waterside. Avoid overcrowded situations, as it might be difficult to notice if a child needs help.

If a child has a seizure, stay calm. From behind, keep their head and face out of the water. If possible, move them to a shallow area, while holding their head above water. Do not restrict movement or place anything in their mouth. Once jerking has stopped, move the child onto dry land. Place them on their side to recover and stay with them until they feel better.

Gross motor delay

Children may need extra support getting to the poolside and into the water and they may need an adult in the water with them. Wheelchair users might consider using canes or walkers if appropriate, and hoists are available at many pools. Young children can usually be carried. It's a good idea to inform the lifeguards, so they can give children appropriate supervision and freedom in the pool, as children often develop swimming styles which appear uncoordinated, even when they have become competent swimmers. A child's physiotherapist will be able to advise on the use of floats, and provide specialized ones if needed.

If children use a wheelchair, it's a good idea to cover the seat with a plastic sheet and a towel, ready for when they get out. Wrap the child in another towel before they sit down to keep them warm and prevent their muscles from going into spasm.

Stretchy waterproof bands can help keep the ears dry, as well as holding ear plugs in place.

Hearing impairment / Deaf

Remove hearing aids before entering the water, unless they are waterproof. It's usually safe for children to swim with cochlear implants, as long as the external part of the aid has been removed, but be sure to check with their specialist first. Silicone ear plugs can help keep water out of the ears, and waterproof headbands can help hold them in place, as well as helping to keep the ears dry. Some doctors may advise against swimming if children have had an operation to insert grommets. Unless a doctor or ENT specialist advises otherwise, children should avoid diving or swimming deep under water, because of the risk of the increased pressure damaging the remaining hearing.

Visual impairment

The echoing sounds within a pool can be very disorientating, so choose a quiet session within a small group. Let children experiment with the water, allowing it to splash on and around them. Before they start learning to swim, make sure they can walk across the pool to understand its width and depth. Encourage them to use rope or lane markings to help them swim in a straight line and check their progress. Use your voice to help them come toward you and use descriptive verbal instructions as well as appropriate touch to guide the children on the correct strokes as they progress.

Front crawl

Front crawl is the fastest and most efficient swimming stroke. It's a good stroke to start with as it follows easily from the dog paddle that children use when they first start swimming and is the most natural to teach and learn.

First things first

It's important to build up the stroke gradually, making sure children master each stage before going on to the next. Firstly concentrate on the body position, next practice the leg kick, then add the arm action and finally the breathing. To keep it interesting, always let children try the whole stroke at the start and end of the practice.

If you can't demonstrate the stroke yourself, find someone who can and get children to look at the pictures in this book. Remember not to spend more than a third of a session on a particular stroke.

Body position

The body should be streamlined and stretched, and as flat as possible, with a slight slope down to the hips and the shoulders resting on the surface of the water. The legs and arms should be stretched, with the toes and fingers relaxed but pointed. The arm action and breathing will cause a certain amount of body roll, but this shouldn't be too exaggerated.

The head should be in a natural position, not lifted or too deep in the water. If it's lifted, the hips and legs will drop too low; if it's buried, they'll be raised too high. The water line should be between the nose and hairline, while the eyes, which should be open, look down and forward.

Body position practices

1. Push and glide from the pool bottom holding a float under each arm or with a noodle under the armpits.

2. Push and glide from the pool bottom holding a float out in front, with the face in the water.

3. Push and glide from the pool bottom without a float, with the face in the water, the arms extended and one hand on top of the other.

How smooth and fast a child's front crawl is depends as much on their body position as on their stroke action. Here are some points to remember:

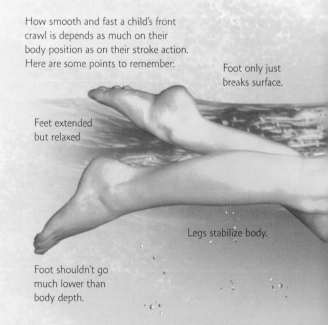

Foot only just breaks surface.

Feet extended but relaxed

Legs stabilize body.

Foot shouldn't go much lower than body depth.

Tip...

If a child is still not interested in putting their face in the water, get them to repeat some of the activities from page 43. Playing some of the games from pages 84–85 might help build up their confidence too.

Leg action

The legs should stabilize the body and provide some forward movement, though most of this comes from the arms.

The legs should kick up and down, alternately and continuously, keeping close together. The movement should start at the hips and end with a whip-like action of the feet. The legs should be kept straight with the feet extended but relaxed. The feet shouldn't go much deeper than the depth of the body on the down-kick and should only just break the surface of the water on the up-kick, making a small splash.

Children usually do six leg kicks per arm cycle, but this isn't important and they will not be able to count them anyway. The opposite leg kicks down at the start of the arm pull, as this helps to balance the body.

Leg action practices

1. Kick, holding on to the wall.

2. Kick, holding a float under each arm, or with a noodle tucked under the armpits.

3. Kick, holding a float out in front, with the chin on the water.

4. Kick, holding a float out in front, with the face in the water.

5. Kick, with arms outstretched, with the face in the water, the arms extended and one hand on top of the other.

Shoulders rest on the surface.

Water line between nose and hairline

Head in natural position, eyes looking forward and down

Legs kick starting at hip.

Body streamlined and stretched

Most of forward movement created by arms.

51

Arm action

Most of the forward movement in front crawl comes from the arm action. This is continuous and alternating, one arm sweeping through the water while the other recovers.

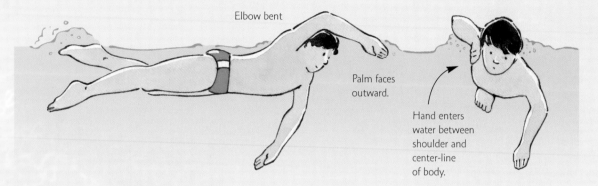

Elbow bent

Palm faces outward.

Hand enters water between shoulder and center-line of body.

The arm enters the water thumb first, with the elbow bent, fingers together and the palm of the hand turned to face diagonally outward.

The hand should enter the water between the shoulder and the center-line of the body.

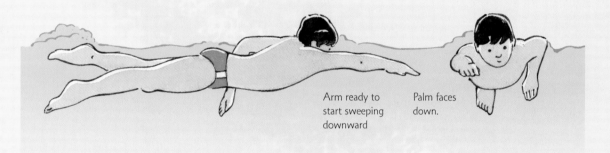

Arm ready to start sweeping downward

Palm faces down.

The wrist and forearm follow the hand into the water and completely submerge then the elbow starts to straighten.

At the same time, the forearm rotates so that the palm is facing down and slightly backward, ready to sweep toward the feet.

Palm faces feet.

Hand close to center-line of body

The arm sweeps downward and backward, with the hand keeping close to the center-line of the body, the palm facing the feet.

The elbow bends again. It must be kept high to ensure that the water is swept backward and not downward.

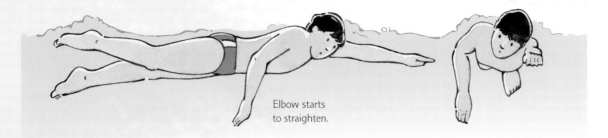

Elbow starts
to straighten.

The hand continues under the body, palm still facing the feet, and sweeps back toward the thigh, with the elbow gradually straightening.

By the time the thumb reaches the thigh, the elbow should be almost completely straight, ready for the last part of the stroke.

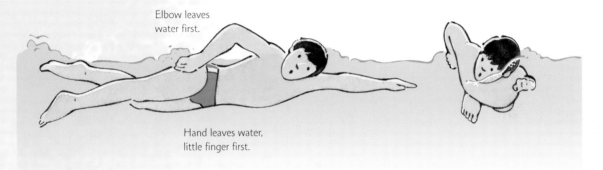

Elbow leaves
water first.

Hand leaves water,
little finger first.

The elbow bends again and is the first part of the arm to leave the water. The arm then swings forward quickly but in a relaxed way.

This part of the stroke doesn't propel the body forward, so as little time and energy as possible should be used on it.

Arm action practices

1. Practice the action standing on the poolside, leaning forward slightly.

2. Practice the action standing in shallow water.

4. Push and glide from the side or the pool bottom, start to kick with the legs, then introduce one or two arm cycles. Increase the number of arm cycles as the stroke improves.

3. Practice the action walking in shallow water.

Push and glide.

Breathing

Breathing should be blended into the stroke with as little interference as possible. The action should be smooth and unhurried.

Action

Breathing out takes place gradually through the nose and mouth, while the face is submerged. The head should turn like a door knob, keeping the body position as streamlined as possible. It doesn't need to be lifted out of the water because the forward motion of the body creates a trough in which to breathe.

Timing

Once the stroke is mastered, children may choose to breathe on both sides, every third arm pull. This method is likely to produce a balanced action. Breathing on both sides also has the advantage of letting swimmers see what is happening on either side of them.

As the hand sweeps back to the thigh, the head turns, ready to breathe in when the elbow comes out of the water.

As the arm swings forward, the breath is taken underneath it.

The head should be back in its normal position before the hand enters the water.

Breathing practices

1. With one hand on the gutter, the other low down on the wall, practice turning the head while kicking.

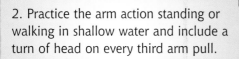

2. Practice the arm action standing or walking in shallow water and include a turn of head on every third arm pull.

3. Kick, while holding a float and practice turning the head to breathe.

4. Practice the full stroke, first holding the breath, then breathing occasionally, then increasing the number of breaths taken.

Tip...

The breath can be let out gradually, forced out all at once just before the next breath in, or released mainly as a trickle and forcing out the last bit of air before taking another breath.

Common faults

Most of the common faults in front crawl come from trying to build up the stroke too quickly, without mastering each stage in turn. Always make sure children can watch the correct action being demonstrated and show them the pictures in the book.

The checklist opposite lists the most common faults and their corrections. When you're correcting a child's stroke, keep your instructions as simple and short as possible. The corrections sometimes need to be exaggerated until they become a habit.

Front crawl checklist

Fault

✗ Kicking too deep. This is caused either by the head being held too high or by a weak kick.

Legs too low

Head too high

✗ Feet come out of the water on the up-kick. The head may be buried too deep or the kick may be coming from the knees.

Kicking from knee

✗ Feet point to the bottom of the pool. This is caused by keeping the ankles rigid and it results in lack of forward movement when kicking.

✗ Kicking with the legs apart.

✗ The hand enters the water across the center-line of the body, so the swimmer "snakes" up the pool.

✗ Slapping the water with the hand.

✗ Pulling too deeply with a straight arm, resulting in lack of power in the arm action.

✗ Not sweeping back with the arm, only down and in, resulting in lack of power.

✗ Not keeping the palm facing the feet, or forgetting to keep the fingers together, resulting in lack of power.

✗ Recovering with the hand too high.

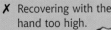

✗ Lifting the head to breathe.

Correction

✓ Practice pushing and gliding with the face in the water.

✓ Practice kicking, holding a float out in front, with the face in the water.

✓ Push and glide. Adjust the position of the head.

✓ Kick, holding a float out in front. Make sure the head is in the correct position. Then practice kicking from the hips with "long legs" and without making a splash.

✓ Kick at the gutter or with a float, keeping the ankles floppy and the toes pointed.

✓ Kick with a float, trying to brush the legs together.

✓ Repeat the arm action practices, trying to enter the water with the hand wide of the shoulder.

✓ Repeat the arm action practices, with the emphasis on "spearing" the water with the hand and putting the thumb in the water first.

✓ Repeat the arm action practices, concentrating on keeping the elbow high and gradually bending it.

✓ Repeat the arm action practices, concentrating on sweeping right through to the thigh.

✓ Repeat the arm action practices, emphasizing "catching" or "fastening onto" the water with the palm and fingers before the start of each sweep.

✓ Repeat the arm action practices, emphasizing that the elbow leaves the water first and remains higher than the hand as the arm swings forward.

✓ Repeat the breathing practices, emphasizing that the head should turn like a door knob and one ear should stay in the water.

Back crawl

Back crawl is a useful stroke for anyone who doesn't like putting their face in the water, or finds the front crawl breathing technique tricky, though some people don't care for it because they can't see where they're going.

One thing at a time

The action for back crawl is basically an upside-down front crawl. It's an easy stroke to teach and learn once the body position has been mastered. Remember that it is important for children to see the correct stroke demonstrated. If you can't do this yourself, enlist the help of someone who can, and show the child the pictures in this book.

Be sure that they build up the stroke gradually, mastering the body position first, then the leg action, arm action and finally the breathing. Spend about a third of a session practicing the stroke, and let children start and end the practice by swimming the whole stroke, to keep their interest.

Body position

The body should be streamlined and stretched, and as flat as possible. Beginners sometimes tend to try sitting up in the water, but this should be avoided. The head should be held still and in line with the body throughout the stroke. The position of the head should be lifted slightly as if supported by a pillow. The ears should be submerged and the eyes should look up and slightly forward toward the feet.

The top part of the body will roll to the side of the pulling arm and this is a natural part of the stroke. The arm action will also make the hips sway from side to side, though this movement should be kept to a minimum by the regular up-and-down action of the legs.

Body position practices

1. Push and glide from the pool bottom, holding one float under each arm.

2. Push and glide from the pool bottom, holding a float on the tummy.

3. Push and glide from the poolside without a float, and arms by the sides.

4. Push and glide from the poolside with arms extended beyond the head.

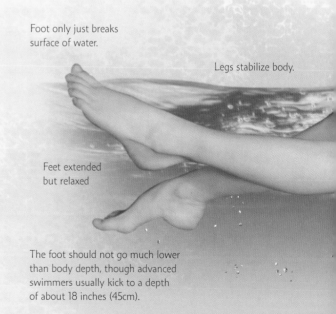

Foot only just breaks surface of water.

Legs stabilize body.

Feet extended but relaxed

The foot should not go much lower than body depth, though advanced swimmers usually kick to a depth of about 18 inches (45cm).

Leg action

As in front crawl, the main function of the legs is to stabilize the body rather than to provide movement.

The legs kick up and down, alternately and continuously, keeping close together. The movement starts at the hips and ends with a whip-like action of the feet. The legs should be kept straight with the feet extended but relaxed. The feet should not go much deeper than the depth of the body on the down-kick and should only just break the surface of the water on the up-kick, making a small splash.

As in front crawl, there are usually six leg kicks to each arm cycle, with the opposite leg kicking down at the start of each arm pull to balance the body. There's no need to worry about timing particularly at this stage though, as this usually comes naturally as the stroke improves. However, it is important to encourage a good kicking action in back crawl, otherwise the body will perform a "snaking" action.

Leg action practices

1. Kick, holding a float under each arm, or with a noodle tucked under the armpits.

2. Kick, holding a float over the tummy.

3. Kick, holding a float over the tops of the knees to stop them from bending.

4. Kick, while sculling with the hands (see page 70 for how to scull).

5. Kick, with the hands on the tops of the thighs.

Tip...

If a child is nervous about lying back in the water, encourage them to push and glide, resting their head on a float or noodle and then practice kicking with the float or noodle in the same position.

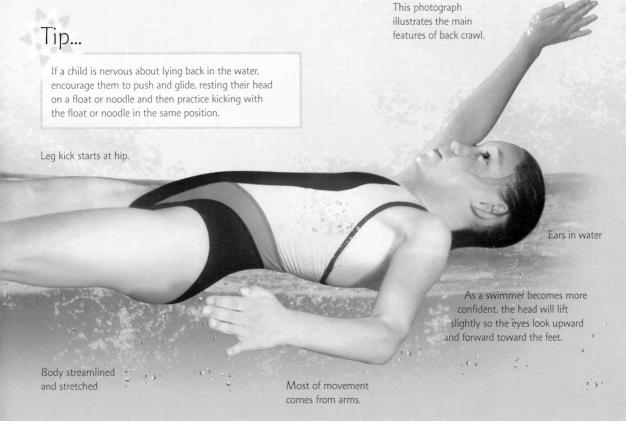

This photograph illustrates the main features of back crawl.

Leg kick starts at hip.

Ears in water

As a swimmer becomes more confident, the head will lift slightly so the eyes look upward and forward toward the feet.

Body streamlined and stretched

Most of movement comes from arms.

Arm action

As in front crawl, most of the propulsion comes from the arms, and the action is continuous and alternating, one arm sweeping through the water while the other recovers. There are two types of arm action.

The straight arm action is often used by beginners and people who swim just for fun. The bent arm action is faster and more powerful. It's used by competitive swimmers, and beginners to whom it comes naturally. Both actions start in the same way.

Start of arm actions

Palm faces outward.

Hand directly behind shoulder

With the arm and hand in a straight line, the arm enters the water directly in line with the shoulder. The little finger enters first, palm facing outward and fingers together. There should be little or no splash. The hand "fastens onto" the water, ready to start the sweep.

Straight arm action

Arm sweeps out to side.

Arm straight

The arm remains straight and starts to sweep. It sweeps outward and slightly downward.

Hand should not go below body depth.

The hand reaches its lowest point at the end of the sweep, when it is level with the shoulder. It should not go below body depth. (The other arm starts to lift at this stage.)

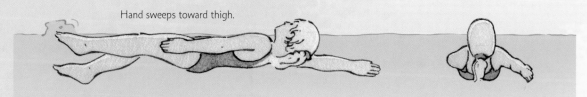

Hand sweeps toward thigh.

The hand continues its semi-circular pathway, sweeping inward toward the hips. The arm remains straight as the hand comes out of the water, back of hand or thumb first.

Bent arm action

Elbow bent

The hand starts to sweep toward the feet. As it does so, the elbow bends and the palm

starts to come into position facing the feet. (The other arm starts to lift out of the water.)

Fingers point upward.

Bend at elbow about 90°.

By the end of the sweep, when the shoulder, elbow and hand are level, the bend at the elbow is about 90°.

At this stage, the other arm is sweeping through the air, over the shoulder, and the palm is turning outward ready to enter.

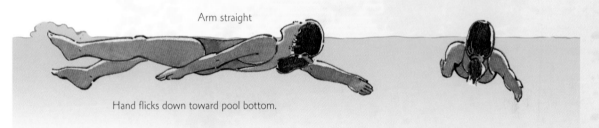

Arm straight

Hand flicks down toward pool bottom.

The hand now sweeps toward the feet and the elbow gradually straightens. The movement ends with a flick of the hand

down toward the pool bottom. This has the effect of raising the shoulder in preparation for the arm leaving the water.

End of arm actions

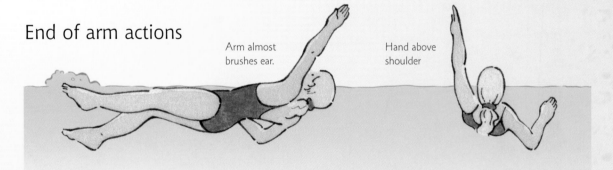

Arm almost brushes ear.

Hand above shoulder

Both actions end in the same way. The arm is lifted smoothly out of the water, straight, with wrist relaxed and the palm facing the thigh.

The arm swings back over the head, almost brushing the ear, the wrist turns so the palm is facing outward ready to reenter the water.

Choosing an arm action style

The action you demonstrate might depend on which one you do yourself. If children are over the age of about six, it may be worth showing them the stronger, bent arm action from the start. If one arm action comes more easily to a child than the other, let them concentrate on that.

Breathing

Breathing in back crawl is fairly relaxed but beginners sometimes tend to hold their breath, so you may need to remind children to breathe normally and regularly. As the stroke improves, encourage them to take a complete breath every stroke cycle.

Arm action practices

1. Practice the arm action standing on the poolside.

2. Push and glide from the side or pool bottom, kick the legs then try one or two arm cycles. Gradually increase the number of arm cycles you make as the stroke improves.

3. Practice the arm action with one arm, holding a float on the tummy. Then practice it with the other arm.

4. Practice swimming the whole stroke with a smooth, continuous arm action.

Breathing practices

Do the full stroke, breathing in on one arm pull and out on the other. Concentrate on smooth, rhythmic breathing and avoid holding the breath.

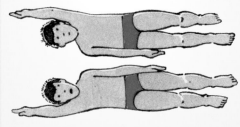

Breathe in.

Breathe out.

Common faults

The best way to avoid faults creeping in is always to master the stroke in stages. Keep any corrections clear and simple, and let children see the correct stroke demonstrated.

Back crawl checklist

Fault	Correction
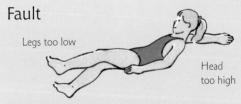 Legs too low / Head too high	✓ Get them to practice pushing and gliding with a noodle under the shoulders, concentrating on putting their head back and their ears in the water. Get them to look up and push their tummy up.
✗ Sitting up in the water is caused by fear of putting the head back. It results in the head being too high and the legs too low.	✓ Kick, holding a float behind the head. (Only use this practice with timid swimmers.)

Back crawl checklist (continued)

Fault

Correction

Legs too high

✗ Putting the head too far back. This is usually caused by trying to look ahead and results in the legs being too high in the water.

✓ Kick, holding a float on the tummy. Put the chin on the chest and look at a fixed point on the poolside.

✗ Kicking from the knees.

✓ Kick, holding a float over the thighs. Concentrate on kicking from the hips with "long legs." The knees should not press against the float.

✗ Kicking with stiff ankles.

✓ Kick, holding a float over the tummy, keeping the ankles floppy and the toes pointed.

✗ Kicking with a lot of splash.

✓ Kick with a float over the tummy. Concentrate on stretching out, putting the head back and keeping the legs under the surface.

✓ Practice the arm action standing on the poolside.

✗ Putting the back of the hand, instead of the little finger, into the water first.

✓ For a short distance, try doing the arm action with one arm only, holding a float under the other arm and kicking with the legs.

✗ Hand enters the water too wide of the shoulder.

✓ Practice the arm action standing on the poolside.

✓ Do a few strokes, trying to enter the water with the hand across the center of the head.

✗ Hand enters the water across the center-line of the body.

✓ Practice the arm action standing on the poolside.

✓ Do a few strokes, trying to enter the water with the hand wide of the shoulder.

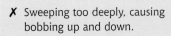

✗ Sweeping too deeply, causing bobbing up and down.

✓ Do a few strokes, concentrating hard on not letting the arm go below body depth.

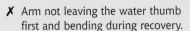

✗ Arm not leaving the water thumb first and bending during recovery.

✓ Practice the arm action on the poolside.

✓ Practice with one arm only for a short distance, holding a float under the other arm.

Breast stroke

This is a popular stroke with people who swim just for fun. It is essential for survival swimming because it's less tiring to swim over long distances than other strokes, and it is used for life saving.

Build up slowly

Remember that it's important for children to see the stroke demonstrated correctly. Be sure that they build up the stroke gradually, starting with the body position, then mastering the leg action, the arm action and finally the breathing. Breathing need not be a problem for beginners, as it's possible to swim the stroke keeping the face out of the water all the time.

Tip...

It's fine for children to swim with their face in the water if it's comfortable. If their legs come out of the water, they can lift their head slightly, which will lower the legs.

One advantage of breast stroke is that swimmers can see where they are going.

Body position

To swim a good breast stroke, the body should be as flat and streamlined as possible. The two sides of the body should be kept symmetrical through the stroke, with the shoulders parallel to the surface of the water. The head should be kept steady and the eyes should look along or just under the surface of the water.

It's harder to achieve this position in breast stroke than in front crawl because the head has to be lifted to breathe and the heels should not break the surface of the water during the leg kick. This means the body is at more of an angle, sloping down from head to feet. The goal is to keep the angle as slight as possible to keep water resistance to a minimum.

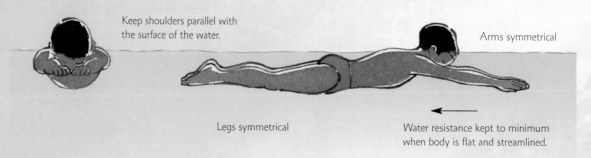

Keep shoulders parallel with the surface of the water.

Arms symmetrical

Legs symmetrical

Water resistance kept to minimum when body is flat and streamlined.

Body position practices

1. Push and glide with a float under each arm or a noodle under the armpits.

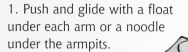

2. Push and glide with a float held in front.

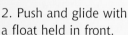

3. Push and glide without a float.

4. Once leg and arm actions have been added, improve the body position by stretching out between each stroke, keeping the arms close to each other and the legs together.

5. Stretch out, putting the face in the water.

Advanced body position

Breast stroke is the slowest of the strokes, so competitive swimmers are always looking for new ways to make it quicker and more efficient. Advanced swimmers learn to undulate like dolphins as they move through the water. To do this, they lift their chest and shoulders out of the water during the arm action, then they dive forward, and glide like a torpedo under water in an outstretched streamlined position for a moment before starting the next stroke.

Keeping the shoulders square throughout the stroke and avoiding moving the head more than needed will help children develop a good technique.

Tip...

Doing the body position practices with a noodle under the armpits will help keep the shoulders and hips level.

Leg action

Much of the forward movement in breast stroke comes from a strong leg kick. There are two types of leg action: the wedge kick and the whip kick. The kick you show to a child might depend on which one you do yourself.

The whip is a faster, more powerful kick. It is used by competitive swimmers but is also suitable for beginners, if it comes naturally to them. The wedge is a slow, relaxed kick used by people who swim just for fun. It is generally a wider kick than the whip and looks more "frog-like."

The whip kick is the easier kick to learn. It can be taught from the start and is the action usually taught to children in classes. If the wedge kick leg action comes more easily to them though, let them concentrate on that at this stage. Gently guiding a child's legs through the kicking motion can help them get used to the correct action, but avoid forcing the action.

Tip...

Try to have both legs doing the same thing at the same time to achieve a smoother stroke.

Whip kick

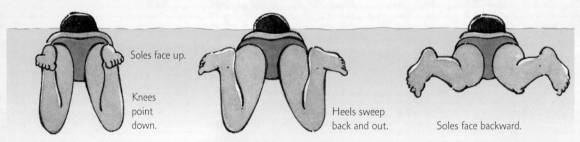

Soles face up.

Knees point down.

Heels sweep back and out.

Soles face backward.

The feet are drawn up to the bottom about hip width apart, with the knees pointing downward to the pool bottom and the soles facing upward.

With the feet turned out, and toes turned toward the shins, the heels sweep mainly backward and slightly outward in a whip-like action.

As the legs straighten, the soles of the feet come into a backward-facing position. The legs are brought together again behind the body.

Wedge kick

Knees point forward and outward.

Soles sweep back and out.

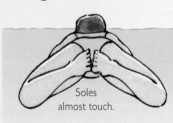  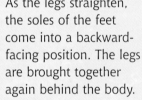

Soles almost touch.

Heels lead.

Heels lead.

The feet are drawn up toward the bottom, with the knees pointing forward and outward and the soles of the feet almost touching.

With the toes turned toward the shins and the heels leading, the soles of the feet then sweep outward and backward.

The legs are straight by the end of the kick. The heels continue to lead as the legs sweep back together again behind the body.

Feet position

The important factor in both types of kick is the position of the feet. They should be turned outward, with the toes turned up toward the shins.

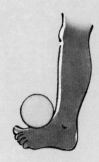

Get children to imagine they are holding a ball between the top of their feet and their shins.

Both kicks start and end with the legs straight out behind the body, feet together and extended but relaxed.

Leg action practices

1. Practice the leg action sitting on the edge of the pool. Start with the legs outstretched, then draw them up toward the bottom. Turn the feet out and the toes toward the shins. Push out to the side, with the heels leading in a circular motion as if around the edges of a hoop, then bring the legs back together again.

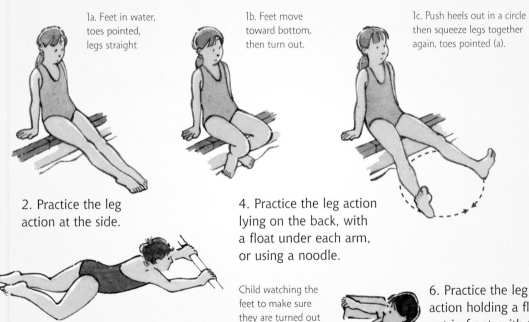

1a. Feet in water, toes pointed, legs straight

1b. Feet move toward bottom, then turn out.

1c. Push heels out in a circle then squeeze legs together again, toes pointed (a).

2. Practice the leg action at the side.

3. Practice the leg action, holding a float under each arm, or with a noodle.

4. Practice the leg action lying on the back, with a float under each arm, or using a noodle.

Child watching the feet to make sure they are turned out

5. Practice the leg action, holding a float out in front, with the chin on the water.

6. Practice the leg action holding a float out in front, with the face in the water.

7. Practice the leg action with the arms outstretched and the face in the water.

Arm action

The breast stroke arm action is a continuous circling movement with a short glide. There are two types of action: the bent arm action, done with the whip kick (see page 64) and the straight arm action, which is done with the wedge kick.

Tip...

Encourage children to look forward as they practice and use the arm action, and to make sure they can see their arms throughout the stroke.

Starting arm actions

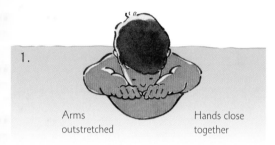

1.

Arms outstretched   Hands close together

Both arm actions start and end in the glide position, with the arms outstretched and the hands close together. As the arms stretch forward, they should be angled slightly down, to about 6 inches (15cm) below the water's surface.

2.

Arm sweep begins.

The palms then turn outward and the arms start to sweep outward, downward and backward until they are just beyond shoulder width apart.

Bent arm action

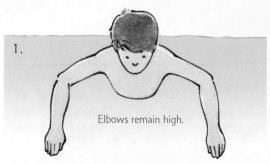

1.

Elbows remain high.

When the hands are just beyond shoulder width apart (see illustration 2, left), the elbows bend but remain high while the hands sweep backward and downward, palms facing the feet and fingers pointing to the pool bottom.

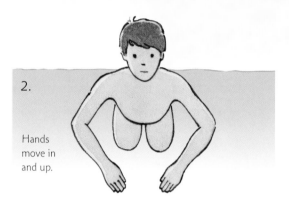

2.

Hands move in and up.

When the hands are underneath the elbows, they start to move together again in a swirling, inward and upward movement. The elbows follow the hands in to the sides of the body.

3.

Hands in prayer position

The palms will probably be in a prayer position or facing upward at the end of this movement. They should be turned downward at the start of the glide.

Straight arm action

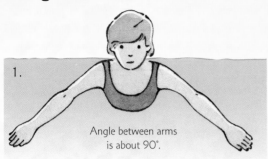

1.

Angle between arms
is about 90°.

When the hands are just beyond shoulder width
apart (see illustration 2 on the page opposite)
the arms remain almost straight and continue
the sweep until they're almost level with the
shoulders and wide of them, and the fingertips
are about 12 inches (30cm) below the surface.

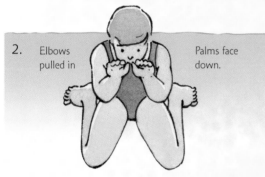

2. Elbows
pulled in

Palms face
down.

The elbows now bend and drop, the hands
are brought together with the palms facing
downward and the elbows are pulled in to the
sides of the body. The arms then stretch
forward smoothly and quickly.

Hands and fingers

Whether children are using the straight arm or
bent arm action, encourage them to keep their
fingers together and palms slightly cupped as
they sweep out to the side. This will help them
to pull through the water.

Aim to create "spoons" –
hands slightly cupped,
fingers together.

Avoid "forks"
– flat hands with
splayed-out fingers.

Arm action practices

1. Practice the arm action standing on
the poolside, leaning forward. The
fingers should be cupped not splayed.

1a. Arms outstretched
and hands together

Bend at
the hips.

1b. Keep
elbows high.

1c. Prayer
position

2. Practice the arm
action standing in
shallow water.

3. Push and glide with the chin on the
water and a noodle under the armpits,
then make an arm stroke. Gradually
increase the number of strokes.

4. Remove the noodle and repeat
practice 3 holding a pull-buoy
between the legs.

Pull-buoy

5. Push and glide from the side with a
noodle under the armpits and with the
chin on the water. Make an arm stroke
and then a leg kick and glide, gradually
increasing the number of strokes.

Breathing and coordination

Once their arms and legs are working well together, children will swim the stroke more efficiently if they put their face in the water for part of the stroke and so reduce the angle of their body.

Breathing and coordination practices

1. Standing in the water, do the arm action and breathe to the front.

2. Practice the leg action, holding a float in front with the face in the water. Every few strokes, raise the head minimally to breathe just as the legs are starting to be drawn up to the bottom.

3. Push and glide from the side of the pool and add one full stroke.

4. Practice the full stroke with the face in the water, increasing the number of breaths taken across the width of the pool.

5. Do the full stroke, breathing every stroke.

6. Count the number of strokes it takes to swim a width, then try to reduce it.

7. Do two arm strokes to one leg kick.

8. Do two leg kicks to one arm stroke.

Remember...

Pull, breathe, kick then glide. While the arms are moving, the legs are streamlined and vice versa.

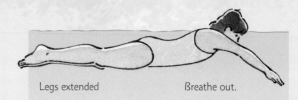

Legs extended   Breathe out.

Breathing out should take place into the water through the mouth and nose during the glide and first part of the arm pull. When the arm action begins, the legs are fully extended.

Legs start to be drawn up.   Breathe in.

A breath is taken at the end of the final sweep of the arm pull and the legs start to be drawn up to the bottom. The head should be raised to breathe by pushing the chin forward the minimum amount needed for the mouth to clear the water.

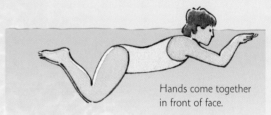

Hands come together in front of face.

The legs continue to be drawn up as the hands come together in front of the face.

Leg kick starts.   Face back in water

As the arms stretch forward, the leg kick starts. The face should be back in the water.

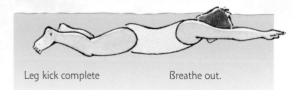

Leg kick complete   Breathe out.

By the time the arms are fully extended, the leg kick is complete.

Common faults

The best way to avoid faults creeping in is to master the stroke in stages. Keep any corrections you have to make clear and simple. Let children see the correct action demonstrated.

Breast stroke checklist

Fault	Correction

✗ The head is held too high out of the water so the hips and legs are too low and the body meets a lot of water resistance.

Water resistance

✔ Do breathing practices.

✔ Push and glide with the chin on the water.

✗ Not kicking symmetrically is caused either by moving the head around or not keeping the shoulders or hips level.

✔ Practice the leg action, first holding a noodle under the armpits or a float under each arm, then holding a float out in front, with the chin on the water. Concentrate on looking ahead, keeping the head steady and the shoulders level. This should keep the hips level. Make sure the knees bend the same amount and in the same direction.

✗ Pointing the feet, instead of turning them out and up.

✔ Push and glide from the side with the feet placed on the wall like a frog's feet.

✔ Pretend to be a frog and jump into the water (at a safe depth) with the feet turned out.

✔ Practice the leg action lying on the back, watching the feet to make sure the heels are pushing back.

✔ Practice the leg action holding a noodle under the armpits, a float under each arm or one float out in front. Focus on pushing back hard with the heels.

✗ Pulling too far back.

✔ Practice the arm action standing up. Make sure the movement takes place in front of the shoulders and that the hands are always in sight.

✗ Bobbing up and down is caused either by bringing the knees too far under the body or by lifting the head too high to breathe.

✔ Practice the leg action with one or two floats or a noodle, ensuring the heels come up to the bottom.

✔ Do the breathing practices, keeping the head and shoulders steady and just pushing the chin forward until it is on the surface of the water.

More water skills

Children can start learning the skills described on these pages at the same time as starting to learn the major strokes. They will add variety and most of them are very useful survival skills.

Tip...

Remember to introduce new water skills one at a time so that children don't get confused.

Sculling

This is an arm action that children can use either to keep afloat in one place or to move gently through the water.

Children should lie flat on their back with their arms by their sides. The arms should be straight but relaxed, with the hands in line with the forearms. The arms then move sideways away from the body with the little fingers raised slightly so that the palms are facing outward and downward. The angle of tilt should be no more than 30°.

The hands shouldn't move more than about 12 inches (30cm) away from the body before turning to come in again. On the inward movement the thumbs should be raised so that the palms face inward and downward.

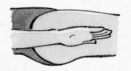 

Palms push away from body.

Palms pull toward body.

This action should be repeated continuously. There should be equal pressure on both outward and inward movements and the movement should start at the shoulders.

Sculling on the spot

To scull on the spot, the action should be made with the palms facing downward.

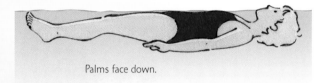

Palms face down.

Sculling head first

To travel head first, the sculling action should be made with the wrists bent upward.

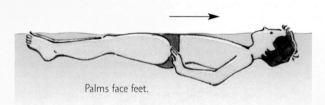

Palms face feet.

Sculling feet first

To travel feet first, the sculling action should be made with the wrists bent downward.

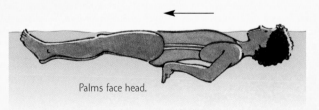

Palms face head.

Tip...

Children may find it helpful to practice with a pull-buoy between their ankles to start with, to keep them afloat.

Sculling practices

1. Practice the arm action standing on the side of the pool.

2. Practice the arm action standing in the pool, with the arms resting on the poolside at shoulder height. Imagine scooping out a hole in sand, using the thumbs on the outward movement and the little fingers on the inward movement.

3. Practice the arm action standing in shoulder depth water with the arms outstretched to the front and submerged. Start off slowly and build up speed.

4. Start the previous practice, then tilt the fingers upward, lie back in the water and continue sculling. Move the hands so that they are alongside the hips. This should produce a head-first scull.

5. Begin as in practice 3, then tilt the fingers downward, lie back and continue sculling to produce a feet-first scull.

6. Begin as in practice 3, then, keeping the palms flat, lie back and continue sculling to produce an on-the-spot scull.

Treading water

A good way of staying in one place in an upright position while using as little energy as possible is to tread water. This is useful if children are in trouble and need to attract attention by waving.

The goal is to keep the mouth and nose above the water by making slow movements. It's a waste of energy to try to hold the body high out of the water. The arms should make gentle sculling actions at chest level, palms facing downward, while the legs do either a breast stroke kick, or a cycling or scissor action.

Treading water practices

1. Practice the leg action with a noodle under the armpits or a float under each arm.

2. Practice, holding on to the side or gutter first with both hands, then with just one hand while the other sculls out to the side.

3. Practice treading water astride a noodle.

4. Practice treading water using the various leg actions, trying to stay afloat for longer each time.

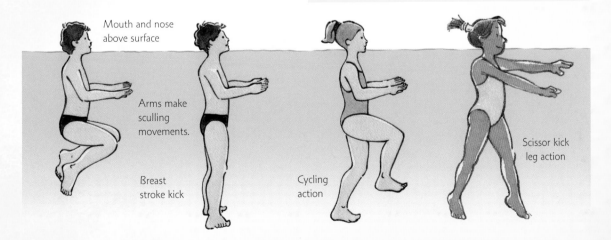

Mouth and nose above surface

Arms make sculling movements.

Breast stroke kick

Cycling action

Scissor kick leg action

Floating

Floating is a vital survival skill that helps children conserve energy if they are in trouble in the water. The floats are shown in what is generally considered to be their order of difficulty. How well each child floats in a particular position depends partly on how they're built, so it's worth them trying all the floats to see which suits best.

The key to successful floating is feeling confident enough to relax completely. Start in shallow water so children can put their feet down quickly if needed. They can move to deeper water as their confidence increases.

Tip...

Encourage children to count during a float and try to float for a little longer each time. They shouldn't hold face-down floats longer than a count of ten before coming up to breathe.

Floating on the back

Children should lie flat on their back with their arms by their sides. They may need to make gentle sculling movements to begin with until they get their balance and feel buoyant in the water. Floating in the star shape shown below will make them even more buoyant.

Children will find floating easier if they keep their head back like this and look up at the ceiling or sky.

Floating on the front

Children should breathe in and lie with their face in the water, either with their arms and legs outstretched or in a star shape. They should lift their head to breathe when they need to.

Lie horizontally.

Mushroom float

Children should lie on their front, take a deep breath in and then tuck up into a ball, hugging their legs with their arms. Their back should be as rounded as possible.

Pull the nose toward the knees.

Floating upright

This needs to be practiced in fairly deep water from the start. After getting into an upright position, the arms should be outstretched, and the head tilted back, so the mouth and nose are just above the surface of the water.

Floating practices

Encourage children to try all the different ways of floating, supported by a noodle, or holding two floats, either at arms' length or under their arms, depending on the float they are doing.

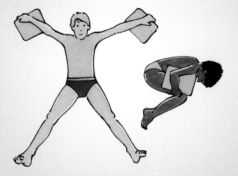

Get them to practice floating with your hand under their back, shoulders or head, gradually reducing the amount of support you give them, and finally removing it, as they gain confidence.

Floating alphabet

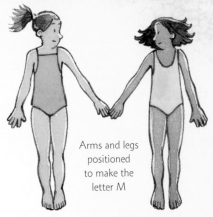

Arms and legs positioned to make the letter M

Once children feel confident floating on their back or front, they could try making different letter shapes, such as a T or Y. This activity can be done in pairs too, to make letters such as A, M or V.

Heat Escape Lessening Position (HELP)

If children get into trouble in cold water, they can improve their chances of survival by keeping their internal organs warm while keeping their head above water (the body loses most heat through the head). They can practice the HELP position by hugging a thick float (or piece of floating debris such as a plastic bottle) with their legs pressed close together and their body suspended straight down, or leaning slightly backward.

In an emergency, a child's clothes can help them conserve body heat, so once children are confident, it can be useful for them to practice this skill wearing a T-shirt and light-weight pants or a skirt.

This girl is in the HELP position with her head above water, legs close together and arms hugging a float to her chest. This would help her survive if she were in trouble in cold water.

Jumping

Once children are confident about jumping into shallow water (of minimum depth 3 feet (1m) or level with the child's armpit when standing on the bottom of the pool) they can start jumping in out of their depth (as long as they know how to come to the surface again). The straddle and tuck jumps described on these pages can be useful if children need to jump into water in an emergency without knowing its depth.

Straight jump

Children should jump up and out from the edge of the pool and enter the water with their body upright, toes pointed and their eyes looking forward. After entering the water, it's important to bend the knees to avoid injuring the spine if they happen to touch the bottom.

When they are doing a straight jump, remind children to point their toes, and make their bodies tall and thin like a pencil.

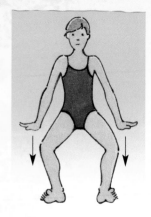

Press down with the palms of the hands.

To surface, children should do a strong breast stroke leg kick and pull their arms down strongly from above their head to their sides, pressing downward with the palms of their hands.

Straddle or step jump

Children should not make this jump from a height of more than 1½ feet (0.5m) above the water or it will be painful. Although it is a shallow jump, to begin with it should be practiced in water that is at least 1½ feet (0.5m) deeper than the height of the child with their arms stretched above their head, to be sure they avoid hitting the pool floor.

Children should step out from the edge of the pool, rather than jump, and enter the water with one foot forward, the other back. The arms should be in front of the body at shoulder level with the elbows bent. The top part of their body should be leaning forward slightly. This position increases the area of their body that hits the water and so prevents them from sinking very far.

As they enter the water, children should keep their legs apart and press the palms of their hands down toward the bottom of the pool. This will also help stop them from sinking.

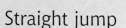

One foot forward, one foot back

Tuck jump

A tuck jump will make a slightly deeper entry into the water but can be made from a greater height than a straddle step. It should be practiced in deep water. As children jump or step off the edge, they should tuck the knees up to the chest, clasping the arms around the legs, so that their bottom hits the water first. Surfacing is the same as for a straight jump.

Tuck to stretch jump

Children should jump up and out with their arms by their sides. At the top of the jump they should tuck their knees up and clasp them with their hands. They should then lift their arms above their head and straighten their body to as near vertical as possible before hitting the water.

Star jump

Children should jump up and out, making a star shape with their arms and legs. Before hitting the water, they should bring their legs together and raise their arms above their head, so their body is as straight and vertical as possible. The star, tuck and stretch jumps will help prepare children for diving head first into the pool.

Climbing out

There might not always be steps around when children need to get out of water, so for safety reasons, they should practice climbing out of the water without a ladder.

As their arms get stronger they can practice pulling themselves up from deeper water, where they won't have the help of a push-off from the bottom.

Put elbows on side.

Pull body up, leaning forward.

Lift one knee onto side.

Start off in shallow water, reach up and put the elbows onto the poolside.

Push off from the pool bottom, lean forward and pull the body up until the arms are straight and supporting the body.

Lift one knee onto the poolside, then bring up the other and stand up.

Surface diving

It can be useful to be able to dive from the surface in an emergency, but children are more likely to use surface dives at the swimming pool for the fun of picking things up from the pool bottom or swimming through someone's legs.

Head-first surface dive

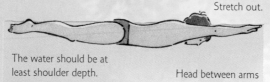

Stretch out.

The water should be at least shoulder depth.

Head between arms

1. Children should take a deep breath and stretch out on their front.

Bend at hips.

Breast stroke arm pull

2. They should make a quick breast stroke arm pull and bend sharply at the hips, forcing the head and shoulders down into the water.

Straighten at hips.

Push arms forward.

Weight of legs drives body down.

Arms in line with body

3. As the legs start to come out of the water, the hips should straighten so the legs are raised into the air. At the same time, the arms should be pushed forward again until they are outstretched in line with the body.

Submerging practices

1. Blow bubbles in the water.

2. Swim through someone's legs.

3. Go down to touch the pool floor.

4. Count how many fingers someone is holding up under the water.

4. Children can go deeper by making another breast stroke pull, but no leg action should be made until the legs and feet are totally submerged.

5. To get into a more horizontal position for swimming under water, the fingers should be turned upward and the head lifted.

Feet-first surface dive

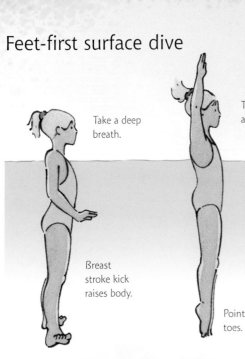

Take a deep breath.

Throw arms above head.

Breast stroke kick raises body.

Point toes.

Lean forward.

Bring knees up.

Tip...

Keep the eyes open under water. Older children who spend longer under water may choose to wear goggles.

Children should tread water (see page 71), then, at the same time, take a deep breath and give a sharp kick to raise their body high out of the water.

With legs together and toes pointed, children should throw their arms above their head, and let their body sink under the water.

Once deep enough, they should draw their knees up to their chest, lean forward and start swimming, keeping their head down to stay under water.

This girl is using breast stroke arm actions and front crawl leg actions to swim under water.

Swimming under water

There are three methods of swimming under water:

- using breast stroke arm and leg action
- using breast stroke arm action with front crawl leg action
- using dog paddle arm action with front crawl leg action

Somersaults

Turning somersaults
in the water is fun and
helps children to develop
confidence. It's also very
good preparation for
diving and learning
to do flip turns.

During a somersault,
keep in a tucked
position with the
back rounded and
the toes pointed.

Forward somersault

Children should start by lying on their front,
doing an on-the-spot scull with their arms,
before raising the head to breathe in.

They should bring their knees up
to their chest and, tucking their
chin down to the knees, press
down with their palms and
start to somersault forward.

Making backward
scooping movements
with their hands will
help children rotate
their body. Encourage
them to imagine they
are turning a jump
rope backward.

Their body should be kept
in a tight tucked position
throughout the somersault,
with the back rounded
and toes pointed.

When the head reaches the surface,
children should start to straighten
out and scull on the spot again,
then raise their head.

Tip...

Hum to prevent
water from going
up the nose.

78

Backward somersault

Children should start on their back, doing an on-the-spot scull with their arms, then breathe in.

Tip...

The tighter the tuck, the faster the somersault will be, so practice getting the knees to touch the chest.

Lifting their bottom and pulling their knees toward their eyes, they should press down with their palms and start to somersault backward.

Somersault practices

1. Practice the tucked position without somersaulting.

2. Push and glide from the side then somersault, on the back or front.

3. Swim breast stroke then somersault forward.

4. Spring off the pool bottom into a somersault.

Making forward scooping movements with their hands will help children rotate their body. Encourage them to imagine they are turning a jump rope forward.

They should keep their body in a tight tucked position throughout the somersault, with their back rounded and toes pointed.

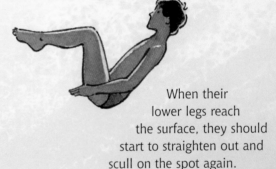

When their lower legs reach the surface, they should start to straighten out and scull on the spot again.

Diving

Diving can add a completely new dimension to a swimming session and offers children a lot of fun and a sense of achievement. Some children take to diving more naturally than others, though, and you should avoid forcing children to dive, as some may find it frightening.

Before you start

Children need to be thoroughly confident about swimming in deep water, jumping into deep water and swimming under water with their eyes open before they start diving. They also need to have good breath control.

Before they start diving properly, they should try the submerging practices described on page 76 and the preliminary practices described on these pages. The submerging, stretching and jumping practices can all be done in the shallow end. The getting into the water practices need to be done in deeper water.

Always make sure the water is deep enough for diving. It needs to be at least 5 feet 10 inches (1.8m) for children attempting the dives described on pages 82–83. Instill in children that their hands must always enter the water first when they dive and that they should keep their heads firmly between their arms, to avoid any risk of head or spine injuries.

Tip...

Encourage children to keep their arms against the ears and to look at their tummy to protect their head and spine.

Jumping practices

1. Jump as high as possible out of the water, keeping the body streamlined and stretched.

2. Jump and dive over a partner's arms, held on the surface of the water.

3. Jump into a handstand in shoulder depth water.

4. Jump as high as possible and turn in the air, keeping the body streamlined and stretched.

5. Jump as high as possible and make different shapes in the air.

Pushing, gliding and stretching under water help children get ready for learning to dive in.

Stretching practices

1. Standing on the poolside, stretch up as tall as possible.

2. Push and glide from the side, turn the head to one side and roll in that direction. Roll from the front to the back and vice versa.

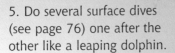

3. Do a mushroom float (see page 72), then stretch out horizontally.

4. Push and glide from the side to the pool bottom, then surface, either by turning the fingers up or lifting the head.

5. Do several surface dives (see page 76) one after the other like a leaping dolphin.

6. Do a handstand in shoulder depth water, concentrating on getting a good stretch.

7. Push and glide from the side into a forward or backward somersault.

Getting into the water practices

Jump into the water from the side of the pool, forward and backward, making different shapes in the air. (See pages 74–75 for jumps and how to surface.) Remember to bend the knees after entering the water, to avoid injuring the spine when landing.

Sitting dive

Children may prefer to dive in from a sitting position to begin with.

One hand clasps the fingers of the other.

Sitting with their feet on the side or gutter, children should extend their arms above their head, clasp one hand with the other and put their chin down to their chest.

Keep arms pressed against ears.

Taking care to keep the arms and head in this position, children should bend forward until they overbalance, lift their hips up and then push off from the side and stretch forward and down.

Kneeling dive

Children may like to start diving with one foot in front of the other. In this case, they should make sure their front foot grips the edge of the pool firmly to avoid slipping. They should progress to a two-footed take-off as soon as possible to avoid dives becoming lop-sided.

Children should go down on one knee at the pool edge with the toes of their front foot gripping the edge, and the toes of their back foot resting on the floor. Their arms, head and hands should be positioned as for the sitting dive.

One hand over the other

They should lean forward until they overbalance, then push off with their front foot and stretch forward and down, taking special care to keep their head down because of the greater height involved.

Eyes looking at tummy

A diver can achieve a streamlined shape like this by keeping their legs together and toes pointed, their head tucked between the arms, and one hand on top of the other.

Crouch dive

Children should crouch on the poolside, with their toes gripping the edge and their arms and head and hands in the same position as before.

This time, when they overbalance and push off, they should try to get their legs straighter and make a less flat entry into the water.

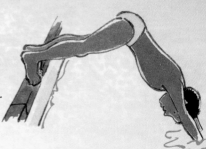

Lunge dive

This is a progression from a kneeling dive.

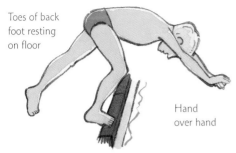

Toes of back foot resting on floor

Hand over hand

For this dive, children should stand on the edge of the pool, with their front leg well bent and their back leg straighter. Their toes should grip the edge firmly. The arms, head and hands should be in the same position as before.

Try to enter the water well away from the side.

They should overbalance and push off with their front leg, at the same time lifting their back leg into the air, then bring both legs together during flight.

Plunge dive

This is a progression from a crouch dive and forms the basis for racing dives.

Look at a point to aim for.

Children should crouch on the edge, looking at the point where they plan to enter the water.

Keep head down and hips up.

They should overbalance forward, swing their arms into position, lower their head and push off vigorously with their feet.

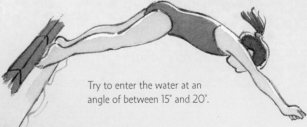

Try to enter the water at an angle of between 15° and 20°.

Children should stretch as fully as they can during flight and keep this streamlined position until their body is totally submerged. To surface, they should tilt their fingers upward and raise their head. Encourage children to glide as far as possible before starting to swim.

Games

Playing games in the water is not only fun and relaxing, but can also encourage children to be more versatile in their movement in water. Here are a few ideas for games to play at the swimming pool.

Playing games

The type of games that can be played in a public pool will depend on its rules and regulations and on how crowded it is. Most of the games described here don't need balls or other equipment as many pools do not allow these except in organized classes.

You will need to supervise all games especially closely; accidents are more likely to happen if children are excited and playing in a group. Children who aren't totally competent when out of their depth should wear armbands.

Most of these games will probably work best with more than the minimum number of players. You may be able to adapt the games, or invent others, to suit the age, ability level and number of children involved. Don't forget the value of action songs and rhymes, especially for younger children (see pages 30–33).

On-the-spot games

These can be played in a small area of the pool.

Simon says (3+ players)

One person is "Simon," who gives instructions such as, "Simon says, 'Blow bubbles!'" Everyone must obey, unless the words "Simon says" are missed out, when they must not. Keep everyone in the game, even if they make a mistake.

Electricity (3+ players)

Players stand in a circle holding hands. One player "switches on" the current by squeezing the hand of the person next to them, who then squeezes the hand of the next person and ducks under the water. This continues around the circle.

These children are playing "kick-of-war," and strengthening their front crawl leg action at the same time.

Safety...

Avoid playing games with balls in waterfront areas. These can be dangerous, as balls tend to float or blow away from the shore and children are tempted to follow them.

Still pond (3+ players)

Everyone floats as still as possible while one person watches. The last one to move wins.

Kick-of-war (2+ players)

Players lie on their front, holding a float between them, then kick to move themselves forward and push their opponent backward.

Races

Children can race individually or in teams. Make sure the teams are evenly matched in terms of ability, and keep the emphasis on having fun.

Skill races (2+ players)

Besides ordinary swimming races and relay races, players can run, jump, hop, side-step or walk on their hands through the water.

Bubble-blowing (2+ players)

Players walk or run, stopping to put their face in the water and blow bubbles every time they have gone an agreed number of paces.

Canoe race (2+ pairs)

Players in each pair stand one behind the other, facing in the same direction, with one noodle tucked under their right arms and another tucked under their left arms. (Small diving rings can be used to pull the ends of the two noodles together into a canoe shape.) Pairs race using front or back crawl leg kick.

Treasure hunt (2+ players)

Individuals, pairs or larger teams race to collect objects such as floats, balls and sinkable toys, and place them in a container or hoop on the side of the pool. This can be played as a race or by allocating points for different objects.

Tunnel swim (2+ players)

Players divide into two teams. Each team stands in line, one player in front of the other, legs apart. The person at the back of each team swims through the team's legs and stands up at the front. The next person then sets off, and so on until each player has swum through the tunnel.

This game is good practice for underwater swimming.

Pair swim (2+ pairs)

Each pair holds hands, then pushes off from the side and swims an agreed distance together, one-handed. Children can play this game with or without floats or noodles.

Shadow swim (2+ pairs)

One partner swims under water, while the other shadows them at the surface.

Try to match speed and stroke style.

Chain scull (2+ pairs)

Players in each pair lie on their back, one behind the other, with the feet of the back player gently resting on the shoulders of the front player. The pairs then scull an agreed distance head first or feet first.

Chasing games

Crows and cranes (3+ players)

Players line up on opposite sides of the pool. One person stands in the middle with a float and calls out the names of two people, one from each side. They have to race to the middle, take the float and try to get it back to their side without their opposite number touching them. A player who is touched gets a penalty point or takes over as the person with the float.

Statues (4+ players)

One player is "it" and the others have to stand still when "it" touches their arm (or other part of their bodies, agreed beforehand). Players can be "unfrozen" by another player touching them or swimming through their legs. The last one caught becomes "it."

Log roll tag (3+ players)

"It" floats or sculls on their back, surrounded by the others who must try to get as close to "it" as possible. "It" suddenly rolls over and tries to catch someone. Whoever is caught becomes "it."

Sharks and minnows (3+ players)

One person is the shark and stands in the middle of the pool. The others are minnows and line up at one side. When the shark shouts "sharks and minnows," they have to try to reach the other side without being caught. Anyone who is caught changes into a shark and helps catch the remaining minnows. The last player to be caught becomes the shark in the next game.

Red letter (3+ players)

"It" stands at one side of the pool, with their eyes shut, and facing away from the rest of the players, who line up on the opposite (home) side. "It" calls out letters of the alphabet; whenever a letter is called out that is in a player's name, that player can take a step forward. The goal is to reach and touch the other side, but when they are getting close, "it" suddenly shouts, "red letter!" turns around and chases them. Anyone who is caught before getting back to the home side becomes "it."

Playing games such as "sharks and minnows" can help children gain confidence in the water.

Swimming in waterfront areas

Waterfront areas such as the ocean or lake can be an excellent place to learn to swim, provided you are extremely careful about safety. Salt water is particularly buoyant, and there is often a large area of shallow water.

Safety...

Tides and currents can make waterfront areas dangerous places, so watch children carefully at all times.

Young children and waterfront areas

Some young children are very frightened of the water and need the same sort of handling as timid children at the pool. Avoid forcing them into the water. Just let them play on the beach, encouraging them gradually to get closer to the water until they're ready to venture in.

Water temperature

Children get cold more quickly than adults because they have less body fat, so they shouldn't stay in the water when they're cold. It's not a good idea to put babies in any but the very warmest water because they have no shiver reflex and can get dangerously cold with no apparent symptoms. The temperature of toddlers and young children also needs to be monitored very carefully.

If children are shivering, get them out of the water right away and wrap them in towels, but don't rub them. It's most important to keep the body's internal organs warm, and rubbing only takes the blood away from them to bring it to the body surface.

Waterfront safety

It is vitally important to take special care about safety in waterfront areas. Follow the rules below and instill them in children. Some of the pool safety precautions also apply to the waterfront.

- Never swim where a warning, for example a red flag, is displayed.

- Don't swim in places without information about the state of tides and currents.

- Never swim unless a competent adult is watching all the time. Young children should have an adult in the water with them.

- Only go out a short way, then swim parallel to the shore. This is especially important if the tide is going out, as it'll be harder to swim back than it was to swim out.

- Don't swim near boats, jet skiers, windsurfers or surfers.

- It's safest not to play on air-beds or in inflatable toy boats. Tides, winds and currents can quickly whip them out to sea or far from the shore.

Coping with emergencies

Routine safety precautions that you should take at swimming pools and waterfront areas are described earlier in the book. On these pages are a few more things to instill in children in case they are ever in trouble. The section also gives some basic advice on how you can help a child having difficulty.

Water safety courses

You are most likely to help others successfully, without putting yourself in unnecessary danger, if you have followed a recognized water safety course. These are available for competent swimmers of all ages: you can find out more information at your local pool, library, or on the Internet.

Try to keep afloat with the minimum of exertion, treading water or adopting the HELP position (see page 73). Treading water can be especially useful because you can wave one arm as you do it to attract attention, as shown here.

If you are having difficulty, tread water and wave to attract attention.

If you are having difficulty

Try to keep calm. If you are near the edge of the water, try to reach it and get out. If you cannot, see if there is anything you can hold on to while you shout for help and wave one arm to attract attention.

Hold on to anything suitable, shout and wave.

If you fall into water with your clothes on, take off anything heavy that will drag you down, such as a jacket, coat or shoes. Light clothes help the body to retain heat, so you should leave those on.

Exerting yourself as little as possible is important, not only to prevent you from getting tired, but also to help keep you warm if you are in cold water, that is, water of less than 77°F (25°C). Any movement will lead to a drop in body temperature by increasing the blood flow to your body surface; this blood is cooled by the water and then circulates around your body, lowering its temperature.

If possible, avoid getting your head wet, too. Unlike most of the rest of your body, your head doesn't have an insulating layer, which means you lose heat from it very quickly.

Tip...

If several people are involved in an emergency, huddle together as closely as possible, depending on the type of floating support available. For example, if you're wearing life jackets, huddle together in a ring, or hold on to a life raft or boat.

Someone else having difficulty

Shout for help or send someone to get help. Don't get into the water yourself if you can possibly rescue the person without doing so. They may be panicking and drag you down with them. Speak to them calmly and keep any instructions clear and simple.

Near the edge

If the person is near the edge of the water, lie down flat, hold on to something secure if possible, and try to grab their wrist (don't let them grab you). Getting down low and grabbing the wrist, rather than the hand, reduces the risk of being dragged in yourself. If anyone else is with you, they should kneel down and hold your legs.

Lie low, hold on to something and grab the wrist of the person in trouble.

If the person is too far out to reach with your hand, quickly look for something to extend your reach: a stick or branch, rope, scarf, towels or clothes, knotted together if necessary. Lie down as you pull the person in.

Hold on to something, lie down and reach out with a branch, rope or clothes.

Farther out

If the person is too far out to reach, throw something that will float, such as a beach ball, rubber ring, or plank of wood for them to hold on to. Don't aim it directly at them but try to make sure it lands within easy reach. Once they are holding the object, tell them either to stay where they are or to try to reach safety by kicking with their legs.

Throw a buoyant object, such as a ball, to a person too far out to reach.

If you're alone, and are a competent swimmer, you may be able to wade in until you're close enough to throw or hold something out to the person. If you hold something out, first lean backward and get a firm foothold to avoid being pulled over.

Rescue key points

- **Summon help.**
  Shout or send for help.

- **Reach.**
  Lie down flat and hold on to something. Reach out to grab the person's wrist. Extend your reach if necessary, for example by using a branch, stick, clothing or rope.

- **Throw.**
  Throw a floating object such as a lifebelt, ball, or piece of wood.

- **Go for help.**
  If help has not already been summoned, go for help. Then come back and reassess the situation.

- **Avoid getting into the water unless you absolutely have to.**

Quite far out in deep water

If you have received proper training in life saving skills, you could swim out to the victim with a floating object. Take off any bulky clothes and your shoes first. Be sure to push the object toward them so that they grab it, not you. Now you can either wait with them until help arrives, go back on your own to get help, or encourage them to swim back with you as they hold on to the object and kick with their legs.

Sculling backward using an upside-down breast stroke leg action will help you supervise and encourage a person in trouble.

As a last resort, it may be possible to give the victim a flotation device or towel to hang on to so you can tow them, swimming on your side or your back.

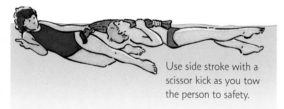

Use side stroke with a scissor kick as you tow the person to safety.

Getting a victim out of water

If the person can't get out of the water on their own and you have received proper training in life saving skills, help them by pushing them out. If they can't manage, tell them to hold on to something and get out yourself. Then, holding their wrist and bending your knees, count to three and pull them out. You may need a second person to help you lift someone who is the same weight as you, or heavier.

Now lift them up over the edge, letting them rest first of all on your extended straight leg before you lower their body gently to the ground. Take care to protect their head as you do this. Now lift their legs over the edge.

Helping a choking baby

If an infant is choking, lay them face down with their head lower than the rest of their body, and give them five sharp blows on the back, with the heel of one hand.

If this is unsuccessful, lie the baby on their back and place two fingertips on their breast bone, a finger's width below the nipples. Give up to five sharp thrusts into the chest. Check the mouth each time. Send for an ambulance and repeat the cycle of back blows and chest thrusts until the baby recovers or help arrives.

If the baby becomes unconscious, start CPR immediately (see page 91) and send for an ambulance if one isn't already on its way.

Helping a choking child

If a child can't clear the obstruction by coughing, lean them forward and give up to five sharp blows between the shoulders.

If this is unsuccessful, stand or kneel behind them, place your fist in their upper abdomen and press sharply into the body and upward up to five times. Give up to another five back blows. Send for an ambulance and repeat the cycle of blows and upper abdomen presses until the child recovers or help arrives.

If the child becomes unconscious, start CPR right away (see page 91) and send for an ambulance if one isn't already on its way.

Resuscitation

If a person is unconscious, it's possible that they're not breathing. Their heart may also have stopped beating. In either case, it is vital you start resuscitation immediately, to get oxygen into their lungs and get the heart pumping the oxygenated blood around their body. The brain suffers particularly quickly from lack of oxygen.

Check for signs of consciousness by gently shaking and shouting at the victim. If they don't respond, check the mouth and clear it of any obstruction, such as seaweed or vomit, if necessary. Use two fingers to tilt the head back with the chin lifted up. (For a baby, use only one finger, making sure you don't tilt the head back too far.) This straightens out the airway and removes the tongue from the back of the throat so they can breathe. Spend up to 10 seconds checking for signs of breathing. If they are breathing, put them in the recovery position (see page 93).

If you can't see, hear or feel them breathing, send for medical help immediately and give two minutes of care. (See "Performing rescue breathing".)

Tilt the head back and lift the chin.

CPR

CPR (cardiopulmonary resuscitation) combines external chest compressions (see page 92) and rescue breathing. You should never perform CPR on a healthy person or a conscious victim.

If the victim is a baby or child, give two rescue breaths, then give them 30 chest compressions alternating with two rescue breaths. If the victim is an adult and help is not already on the way, go for help, then come back and give CPR, starting with two breaths and follow with 30 chest compressions. Keep going with CPR until help arrives, you are exhausted or the victim recovers. If normal breathing returns, put them in the recovery position (see page 93).

Performing rescue breathing

Check for breathing. If the victim is not breathing, and they are **a baby or child**, keep the head tilted back, open the mouth, then seal your lips around the mouth and nose, and breathe into their lungs gently and steadily, watching their chest rise as the lungs are filled with air. (Blow from your cheeks rather than breathing deeply from your lungs.)

Mouth covers baby's mouth and nose.

For **a larger child or an adult** who is not breathing, keep the head tilted back, open the mouth with one hand and with your other hand pinch the nostrils firmly together. Seal your lips around the mouth and breathe into the lungs slowly and steadily, watching the chest rise as the lungs are filled with air.

Mouth covers mouth only.

When the chest falls, put in the next breath.

You may need to start rescue breathing while you're still in the water. If you're within your depth, try to support the victim's body with one arm, use two fingers to hold their chin shut, closing the mouth, and blow into the nose.

Mouth covers victim's nose.

Remember...

You may need to adjust your technique depending on the size of the victim. For example, rescue breaths should preferably be given to a child through the mouth, but if your mouth covers the mouth and nose of a small child, then this method would be most appropriate.

Performing chest compressions

Lie the victim on their back on a firm surface while you kneel alongside, facing their chest and in line with the heart. Pressure needs to be applied to the breastbone. Performed incorrectly, chest compressions can injure the victim further, so it is important to press in the center of the victim's chest.

Babies and small children

For infants, use very gentle pressure with two fingers. Press at a rate of 100 times per minute to a depth of ½–1 inch (1–2.5cm).

For small children, use light pressure with the heel of one hand. Press at a rate of 100 times per minute to a depth of 1–1½ inches (2.5–4cm).

Children and adults

Place the heel of one hand in the center of the chest. Place the heel of the other hand on top and interlock your fingers to hold them away from the victim's body. Push straight down 1–1½ inches (2.5–4cm) for children, 1½–2 inches (4–5cm) for adults. Lock your elbows and use your upper body to perform compressions. Keep your hands on their chest. Try to give 100 compressions per minute.

Remember...

You may need to adjust your technique depending on the size of the victim. For example you may find you need to use one hand, rather than two, to give chest compressions to a smaller child, making this method most appropriate.

Resuscitation key points

- **Remove victim from danger.**

- **Check response.**
  Does victim respond to speech and touch?

- **Summon help.**
  If victim responds, put them in the recovery position and go for help.
  If there is no response, shout for help.

- **Open the airway.**
  Tilt the head, clear obstructions, lift the chin.

- **Check breathing** (for up to 10 seconds).
  Look, listen and feel for signs.

- **No breathing – give rescue breaths.**
  Give **1 breath every three seconds** to babies and children. (If an adult is not breathing and help is not on its way, go for help now. Then return and start CPR with 30 chest compressions. If help is on its way, start CPR with 30 chest compressions.)

- **Still no breathing – start CPR.**
  Perform chest compressions in the center of the chest.

- **Babies and small children**
  Use two or three fingers for **babies** at a depth of ½–1inch (1–2.5cm).
  Use the heel of the hand for **small children** at a depth of 1–1½ inches (2.5–4cm).
  30 compressions: 2 breaths
  100 compressions per minute

  Give CPR for 2 minutes then, if help is not already on its way, go for help (you can take a baby or small child with you). If you have to leave a child to go for help, continue CPR as soon as you return.

- **Children and adults**
  Use clasped hands at a depth of:
  1–1½ inches (2.5–4cm) for **children**.
  1½–2 inches (4–5cm) for **adults**.
  30 compressions: 2 breaths
  100 compressions per minute

- **Stop CPR when:**
  Help arrives.
  You are exhausted.
  Victim recovers.

The recovery position

An unconscious person who is breathing and whose heart is beating should be put in the recovery position. By doing this, you will help to keep their airway clear so they can breathe easily and will not choke. (People often vomit before they lapse into, or as they come around from, unconsciousness.)

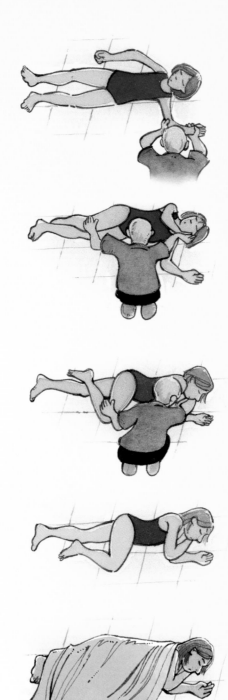

1. Straighten the legs and place the arm nearest to you at right angles to the body, with the palm upward.

2. Bring their other arm across the chest and hold the palm against the cheek to support the victim's head while you turn them. (Turn scratchy rings away from their face.) Hold the leg furthest away from you above the knee and lift it toward you. The leg will bend while the foot stays on the floor.

3. Keeping hold of the victim's knee and supporting the head, use the leg as a lever to help roll them over toward you. Adjust the victim's upper leg if necessary, so the hip and knee are both bent at right angles.

4. Tilt the chin forward to keep the tongue clear of the airway. Adjust the position of the hand under the cheek if you need to.

5. Cover the victim with a coat or towel to keep them warm.

Going further

Swimming classes are an excellent way to help children become more confident in the water and improve their skills. There are classes for children of different ages and levels of ability.

Classes and clubs

Going to classes and clubs can improve children's swimming and fitness and give them the chance to meet other swimmers. They can provide information about the many nationally recognized awards that children can take at different levels and in different types of swimming. Classes and clubs can also help children follow up or develop an interest in a particular aspect of swimming – perhaps learning life saving or diving, or taking up synchronized swimming, water polo, or open water swimming.

Finding information

The best place to find out about classes and clubs in your area is from the notice board at your local swimming pool. The local parks department should also have lists on their websites, and libraries may have information too. Remember to make sure that any class or club is run by certified instructors.

Joining a swimming class or club can help children develop their swimming skills, make new friends and form part of a healthy lifestyle.

Internet links

The Internet is a good source of information about local swimming pools and teaching your child to swim. At the Usborne Quicklinks Website we have created links to websites you may find useful.

To visit the sites, go to **www.usborne-quicklinks.com** and type the keyword "swim". Here are some of the things you can do on the Internet:

- Look for baby-friendly swimming pools in your area.
- Watch animated demonstrations of strokes.
- Brush up on the words and tunes to action songs and nursery rhymes.

Internet safety

The websites recommended in Usborne Quicklinks are regularly reviewed. However, the content of a website may change at any time and Usborne Publishing is not responsible for the content of websites other than its own. We recommend that children are supervised while on the Internet.

Index

Photography credits

Every effort has been made to trace the copyright holders of the material in this book.
If any rights have been omitted, the publishers offer to rectify this in any future edition,
following notification. The publishers are grateful to the following organizations and
individuals for their contribution and permission to reproduce this material.

Usborne Publishing is particularly grateful to:
Amateur Swimming Association
Delphin Swim Discs
Down's Syndrome Association
Floaties (www.qpie.co.uk)
Jaco Enterprises, Inc.
Kushies®
Swimshop®
Zoggs International Ltd

(t = top, m = middle, b = bottom, l = left, r = right)
4 © Daniella Boutin; 6b © Daniella Boutin; 7t Profimedia.CZ s.r.o/Alamy; 8b LWA-Dann Tardif/CORBIS;
10b David Oliver/Stone/Getty Images; 11b © Usborne Publishing Ltd; 12t © Usborne Publishing Ltd;
13b Taxi/Getty Images; 14t Creatas/Oxford Scientific; 15b Profimedia.CZ s.r.o./Alamy; 16b Stockbyte Gold/Getty
Images; 16mrt Kushies Swim Nappy © Kushies®; 16mrb Floaties Standard Aquanappy © Incy Wincy,
info@incywincy.net, Tel. 0118 3773 581, www.incywincy.net; 17t © Daniella Boutin;
18b RubberBall/Imagestate; 19bl © Usborne Publishing Ltd, courtesy of Delphin Swim Discs
www.schwimmscheiben.de; 19br © Early Learning Centre; 19m © Usborne Publishing Ltd;
19t Vstock/Alamy; 20b © Daniella Boutin; 20mr Zoggs Pull Buoy, courtesy of Zoggs International Ltd,
www.zoggs.com; 20tl photograph included by kind permission of the ASA; 20tr Win Swim Belt courtesy
of Swimshop® www.swimshop.co.uk; 21t © Daniella Boutin; 22b Profimedia.CZ s.r.o./Alamy;
23tr RubberBall/Alamy; 24b ACE STOCK LIMITED/Alamy; 26b Roy Ooms/Masterfile www.masterfile.com;
28 © Daniella Boutin; 30t © Daniella Boutin; 32b Profimedia.CZ s.r.o./Alamy; 34b Tim Kiusalaas/Masterfile
www.masterfile.com; 37 © Daniella Boutin; 39b Profimedia.CZ s.r.o./Alamy; 40b © Daniella Boutin;
42b © Daniella Boutin; 44t © Daniella Boutin; 45b Zac Macaulay/The Image Bank/Getty Images;
47b Profimedia.CZ s.r.o./Alamy; 48b © Down's Syndrome Association; 49t Ear Band-It® headband
photo courtesy of Jaco Enterprises, Inc., Phoenix, AZ, www.earbandit.com; 50&51b © Daniella Boutin;
56&57b © Daniella Boutin; 62m © Daniella Boutin; 63b © Daniella Boutin; 72b photograph included by
kind permission of the ASA; 73b © Daniella Boutin; 74 © Daniella Boutin; 77b David Nardini/Masterfile
www.masterfile.com; 78 © Daniella Boutin; 81t David Nardini/Masterfile www.masterfile.com;
82&83 © Daniella Boutin; 84b © Daniella Boutin; 86b © Daniella Boutin;
94b Candice Farmer/Taxi/Getty Images

Usborne Publishing is not responsible and does not accept liability for the availability or content of any website
other than its own, or for any exposure to harmful, offensive, or inaccurate material which may appear
on the Web. Usborne Publishing will have no liability for any damage or loss caused by viruses that
may be downloaded as a result of browsing the sites it recommends.

This revised edition published in 2006 by Usborne Publishing Ltd,
Usborne House, 83-85 Saffron Hill, London EC1N 8RT, England.
www.usborne.com First published in America in 2007. AE.